The Ghosts of the British Isles: A Collection of Ghost Stories and Other Supernatural Tales from Britain and Ireland

By Charles River Editors

A page from *Bald's Leechbook*

About Charles River Editors

Charles River Editors is a boutique digital publishing company, specializing in bringing history back to life with educational and engaging books on a wide range of topics. Keep up to date with our new and free offerings with [this 5 second sign up on our weekly mailing list](), and visit [Our Kindle Author Page]() to see other recently published Kindle titles.

We make these books for you and always want to know our readers' opinions, so we encourage you to leave reviews and look forward to publishing new and exciting titles each week.

About the Author

Sean McLachlan spent many years working as an archaeologist in Europe, the Middle East, and the United States. Now a full-time writer, he's the author of many history books and novels, including *A Fine Likeness*, a Civil War novel with a touch of the paranormal. Feel free to visit him on his Amazon page and blog.

Introduction

An Anglo-Saxon belt buckle depicting the god Woden (Odin)

Ghost Tales of the United Kingdom

"In Scotland, beautiful as it is, it was always raining. Even when it wasn't raining, it was about to rain, or had just rained. It's a very angry sky." – Colin Hay

The United Kingdom is an ancient land steeped in history and tradition, filled with prehistoric ruins, majestic castles, and a countryside sculpted from millennia of human habitation. Its rolling countryside is dotted with prehistoric burial mounds and stone circles. Brooding castles hold tales of bloodshed and honor. Medieval churches have elaborate stained glass windows and gruesome carvings, reflecting a mixture of hope and darkness. Every hamlet and village has tales that go back centuries, and folk festivals with roots in pagan times.

Thus, it is not surprising that many believe the area is filled with ghosts. For centuries, people have told tales of ghosts stalking its historic buildings, strange creatures lurking in its primeval forests, and unexplained paths linking its ancient sites.

Scotland is a fascinating and ancient land filled with history. It has produced explorers, warriors, inventors, writers, and more than a few murderers. For many centuries, it fought bitter wars against England to maintain its independence, and even when those wars were finally lost, Scotland retained its distinct culture and identity. Though a part of the United Kingdom, it would be a mistake to lump it in with England, Wales, and Northern Ireland, as Scotland has its own tales to tell and traditions to maintain. Not everything in Scotland is as it appears, however. Some Scots say this is a land haunted by spirits, a place of strange disappearances and unexplained phenomena. There is no shortage when it comes to the strange stories Scotland has to offer, and the legends and lore have compelled many to dig a little deeper and even explore this wonderful land for themselves. Some of those tales are downright grisly. Scotland has always been a rival to its southern neighbor, and the rivalry extends to the number of hauntings in its medieval castles, stately homes, and old cobblestone streets. While many Englishmen claim that their country is the most haunted, the Scots can point to their own stories of ghosts as evidence they may beat the English in this dubious distinction.

The Welsh have their distinct language and customs and have always felt themselves to be a people apart from the neighboring English. This division goes back to the 5th century, when the ancient Britons fled west in the face of the Anglo-Saxon incursion. The Anglo-Saxons were made up of three tribes—the Angles, Saxons, and Jutes—from what is now Denmark and northern Germany. These tribes took advantage of the Roman legion's departure to attack vulnerable Britons, taking over England until the Britons in Wales defied them. This defiance continued into the Middle Ages, and numerous wars occurred as successive English kings tried and eventually succeeded in asserting their will over the rebellious country. With such a storied and violent past, it is no surprise that Wales has many tales of ghosts.

Ireland is an ancient land, filled with prehistoric ruins, age-old traditions, and a rich and abiding folklore. Many of the old Irish traditions and tales dwell upon the world beyond our own, the shadow world of spirits. Every village and landmark has a tale attached to it, a good many of them rooted in pagan beliefs from prehistoric times. Others are more modern, and deal with historic tragedies such as the English invasion, the Potato Famine, or the Troubles. According to some locals, ghosts seem to haunt every historic building and place, acting as symbols of the past that still haunts this troubled land. For example, at Aughagreagh in County Longford there's a wall running alongside a road. It's just a typical drystone wall like so many in Ireland used to show the boundary of a farmer's field. The road is just a typical road. But sometimes at night passersby will see a woman and two small children sitting on this wall. They wear tattered clothing in the style of the 19th century. Their faces are drawn and emaciated, their eyes sunken. They have a look of hopeless resignation about them. This is because they are famine victims.

The wall stands on the road to the old workhouse, where Ireland's poor and starving were packed into cold rooms and forced to work long hours of hard labor in exchange for a crust of bread and constant abuse. They were literally punished for being poor, and their spirits have remained in this sad place.

Ireland also has a rich folklore. Everyone knows about the fairy folk and leprechauns and many have heard of the fearsome banshee. The stranger side of the Emerald Isle goes much deeper than that, however, with tales of phantom armies marching through the sky, sea monsters swimming in the waters around the island, and stories of strange powers and dark magic. Indeed, these tales are not consigned to the past; many unexplained occurrences continue to happen, even today. Here is a sampling of some of the Emerald Isle's better-known ghosts, plus a few obscure ones. They represent just a small portion of the hundreds of restless spirits that haunt this troubled land. For the purposes of this book we are covering the entire island, including Northern Ireland.

The Ghosts of the British Isles: A Collection of Ghost Stories and Other Supernatural Tales from Britain and Ireland looks at various ghost stories and unexplained phenomena that make the British Isles such an intriguing place. Along with pictures of important people, places, and events, you will learn about the ghosts of the British Isles like never before.

The Ghosts of the British Isles: A Collection of Ghost Stories and Other Supernatural Tales from Britain and Ireland

About Charles River Editors

About the Author

Introduction

   Early English Hauntings

   The Most Haunted House in England

   The Most Haunted House in London

   Haunted Churches in England

   Haunted Ruins in England

   Haunted Castles in England

   Haunted Graveyards across England

   Haunted Welsh Castles

   Haunted Welsh Houses

   Haunted Welsh Inns and Pubs

   Wales' Traveling Ghosts

   Wales' Violent Spirits

   The Pit of Ghosts

   Just Plain Weird

   Haunted Castles

   Haunted Roads

   Edinburgh

   Haunted Pubs and Churches

   Remote Ghosts

   Early Irish Hauntings

   Ireland's Haunted Castles

   Ireland's Other Haunted Historic Buildings

   Haunted Irish Graveyards

   Haunted Houses

   Other Haunted Places

   Online Resources

   Further Reading

Free Books by Charles River Editors

Discounted Books by Charles River Editors

Early English Hauntings

England has been haunted for nearly all of its recorded history. The earliest account of ghosts in the country dates to the Middle Ages. During that time, there was a deeply held belief in the existence of Purgatory, a place between Heaven and Hell where the dead might stay for a time to suffer the torments of Hell before being forgiven and sent to Heaven. Few people were good enough to go straight to Heaven, or so bad as to go right to Hell, so most ended up in Purgatory. Their loved ones would then light candles, say prayers, and pay the local clergy to hold masses in their honor, which helped shorten the spirits' time of suffering. Wealthy people often set money aside in their wills to pay for these services.

At other times, the spirits of the dead would appear to their relatives, asking for help to be released from Purgatory. In 1457, one Englishman saw an apparition of his recently deceased uncle telling him to go on a pilgrimage to the famous shrine of Santiago de Compostela in Spain to say a mass for him there. Only then would the dead man ascend to Heaven.

These were not just folktales or stories told from the pulpit. Perhaps the earliest firsthand eyewitness account of a ghostly encounter comes from a 15th century commonplace book, a combination of a diary and repository for interesting facts and quotes. The man who had kept it, quite matter-of-factly, told how the "dark shadow" of his deceased mistress had appeared to him and said, "I can be freed from the punishment I am suffering if masses were said for me by good priests."

The best collection of medieval ghost stories comes from Byland Abbey in North Yorkshire. Around the year 1400, a monk wrote several local ghost tales down. The ghosts in the stories generally communicated with the living to seek absolution, as in the following tale:

> "This concerns the ghost of a hired servant from Rievaulx who helped a man carry beans. The story goes that a man was riding his horse carrying a peck of beans. His horse stumbled on the road and broke its leg. When the man noticed this, he carried the beans on his back and while he was walking, he saw something like a horse standing on its hind legs, its forelegs raised high. The terrified man invoked the name of Jesus Christ, praying the horse would do him no harm. This done, the apparition walked with him as if it were a horse. After a while, it appeared in the shape of a revolving bale of hay with a light in the middle to which the living man said, 'God forbid that you bring evil on me.'

> "After he said this, it appeared in the shape of a man. The ghost told him his name and added, 'Allow me to carry the beans to help you.' And he did this all the way to a river, but he did not want to cross beyond it, and the living man did not know how the sack of beans had been placed on his own back once more. Afterward, he made sure the ghost was absolved and that masses were sung on the ghost's behalf so that the

ghost was helped."

Ghosts were also known to appear to remedy earthly injustice.

"Concerning the sister of Adam de Lond of a former time who had been caught after her death, according to an ancient report:

"The aforementioned woman was buried in the cemetery of Ampleford. A short time afterward, she was caught by the elder William Trower and having been conjured, she confessed she had traveled her own road at night on account of certain property deeds that she had unfairly given to her brother, Adam. This was because a certain discord had arisen between her husband and herself, and with injustice to her husband and her own sons, she offered the deeds to her brother.

"Thus it was that after her death, her brother violently expelled her husband from her home, evidently from one toft [a house and its adjoining arable land] and crofte [tenant farm, garden, or pasture] with appurtenances in Ampleford and in Heslarton from one bovata [15 acres] of land with appurtenances. Therefore, she begged William that he advise the brother that she wished to return the deeds to her husband and sons and restore her land to them. This was the only way she would be able to rest in peace before Judgment Day. Thus William advised Adam, but he refused to restore the deeds, saying, 'I do not believe the things you said.' William replied, 'My speech is true in all things. God willing, you will hear your sister talking with you about this matter soon.'

"On the next night, he again caught her, brought her to Adam's bedroom, and she spoke to him. Then, her hardened brother replied, 'Even if you will have wandered about in perpetuity, I am not willing to return the deeds.' She replied with a heavy sigh, 'May God judge between you and me on this matter. You should know that because of this, up to your death I shall not rest. And after your death, you will wonder about in my place.'

"The right hand of that woman was hanging downward and was exceedingly black. And she was asked about the cause, she responded that very often, when arguing, she extended it for the purpose of swearing falsely. Finally, she was conjured to another place because of the nightly fear and terror of the people of the village. I seek pardon, nevertheless, if by chance I have offended in writing contrary to the truth. Nevertheless, it is told that Adam de Lond Junior did, in fact, made reparation of some of the inherited property after the death of Adam Senior."

WyrdLand.com's picture of Byland Abbey

As can be seen, England has been a haunted place since at least the Middle Ages. Perhaps the Romans saw ghosts there, too, as they certainly believed in them. Sadly, no accounts from Roman Britain have been found, although some Roman spirits certainly have.

Hampton Court Palace, home to 500 years of royalty, is said to have several ghosts. The most famous is Catherine Howard, the fifth wife of Henry VIII. Catherine was still a teenager when she married an obese and, some say, impotent king. It wasn't long before Henry accused her of having an affair with the courtier Thomas Culpeper and put her under house arrest. The two had flirted before her marriage to the king, so these accusations may have been true or may have been the result of an increasingly moody and jealous monarch. She was confined to her quarters, but one day she managed to break free from her guards and ran down one of the palace hallways towards a room where Henry was praying, hoping to beg for her life. Before she could see the king, the guards grabbed her and dragged her back to her quarters as she screamed and struggled. She was later beheaded in the Tower of London. According to rumor, her last words were, "I die a Queen, but I would rather have died the wife of Culpeper." Centuries later, in this same hallway, generations of visitors and palace staff have heard screams at all hours of the day and night as the teenage queen's terror supposedly echoes down the centuries. For more than a hundred years it has been known as the Haunted Gallery.

Catherine Howard

Another of Henry's wives, who managed to die of natural causes, Jane Seymour, is also said to haunt the palace. In 1537 she gave birth to Henry's first son after years of disappointment and two previous wives not providing him with an heir. The future King Edward VI was born healthy, but his mother suffered complications from the delivery and died shortly after giving birth. A distraught Henry wrote to the king of France, "Divine Providence…hath mingled my joy with bitterness of the death of her who brought me this happiness."

Jane Seymour

The room where she died is at the top of the Silver Stick Stairs, named after the sign of office of one of the king's attendants. Every year around the anniversary of Seymour's death, a ghostly apparition of a woman dressed all in white is seen passing down the stairs holding a candle, heading for the rooms where her infant had his nursery.

The palace seems to be getting new ghosts as well. One, dubbed by the press as "Skeletor", made his appearance as recently as 2003. For three consecutive days, a CCTV camera caught a set of fire doors flying violently open. On the first day there was no apparent cause. On the second day they burst open, a strange, elongated male figure in what appeared to be Tudor era dress passed into the doorway from the inside and then closed the doors. The next day the doors again flew open, but this time Skeletor did not make an appearance. What's interesting is that when the doors burst open on the second day, Skeletor wasn't behind them; the doors, like on the other days, opened all by themselves. The purported ghost only closed them. The palace as CCTV cameras in countless locations and the figure wasn't seen approaching or leaving the area. He came out of nowhere, and vanished just as abruptly.

In London, another popular tourist attraction is the British Museum. Although visitors flock there to see its Egyptian mummies, there's a very English mummy not far off in University College on Gower Street. One of the cofounders of the college was Jeremy Bentham (1748-1832), who felt that Christian burial was a pointless waste and that corpses should be used for scientific investigation and then preserved as a monument. True to his word, he left orders in his will to be publicly dissected and then mummified. His dissection was performed during a fierce thunderstorm that some traditionalists interpreted as the wrath of God. Nevertheless it was well attended by his friends.

Bentham

However, his mummification did not go so well. The doctors tried to imitate a Maori recipe for mummification but the head turned out a hideous mess, with blackened, leathery skin that did not resemble the jowly Englishman in the least. So the doctors cut off his head and replaced it with a wax model topped with Bentham's own hair. The body was then dressed in his clothes, complete with his favorite walking stick and seated in an "auto-icon", a glass-fronted cabinet in the university. His head was placed to his side but later put under lock and key when some students were caught playing football with it.

At times, students whisper, Bentham leaves his case and can be seen walking down the hall. Sometimes he's not seen, but the rhythmic tapping of his walking stick signals that his spirit is on the move. Perhaps it is restless, and Bentham should have opted for a more traditional burial.

The Most Haunted House in England

England has many haunted houses. It seems that every historic home—and even some modern ones—has a ghost in residence. Having traveled the length and breadth of England, it is hard to go to a single town or village however small where locals did not claim a house was haunted.

That said, Borley Rectory in Essex is the only one that has earned the title of "the most haunted house in England." A Gothic Revival home built in 1862 for the rector of the village of Borley, it became notorious in the first decades of the 20th century for a spate of ghostly encounters.

The rectory

While the house itself is rather new by English standards, the village of Borley dates back to Anglo-Saxon times, and there are several medieval buildings in the area. The church the rectory serves dates to the late 12th century. An earlier rectory that burned down in 1841 had previously stood on the site, and that earlier building was built upon medieval foundations itself.

After the rectory was finished, the Reverend Henry Dawson Ellis Bull moved in as its first resident along with his wife and children, who eventually numbered 14. Within a year, strange occurrences were reported by the reverend's children, as well as locals visiting the house. At first, these were minor in nature, such as the sound of footsteps in rooms when no one was there. Then, in 1885, the headmaster of a local grammar school saw the ghostly figure of a nun walking the grounds on numerous occasions. Guests who attended dinner parties at the rectory often reported the pale face of a nun peering in through the window at them.

The Reverend Bull died in 1892, and his post was taken over by one of his sons, the Reverend Henry "Harry" Foyster Bull. It was during his tenure at the house that the manifestations became stronger. On July 28, 1900, four of the rector's daughters were strolling the grounds in the early evening when they saw the ghost of a nun not far from the house. When they tried to speak to her, the apparition disappeared. Other sightings occurred in the house and on the grounds, and it wasn't long before the entire large family was convinced the rectory was haunted by a number of ghosts.

Locals and visitors to the church had spotted them, too. Many saw the nun, and some had also seen her accompanied by a monk with a tonsured head and long black cloak. Several claimed to have seen a phantom carriage driven by two headless men. This particular sighting sounds more like folklore than a modern haunting; the headless horsemen motif is an old one, dating back to at least the Middle Ages and perhaps as far back as Celtic times, when there were cults to decapitated heads and warrior's chariots were adorned with the heads of one's enemies (which was considered the epitome of bravery). Usually, the headless horsemen either ride a black horse or drive a black coach. Sometimes the horses are headless, too. People have claimed to see headless horsemen and coachmen throughout the British Isles, usually scaring lone travelers at night. To find one riding through the middle of a village is less common.

The hauntings increased during the tenure of the next rector, the Reverend Guy Eric Smith, who took over in 1929. On their first day in the house, the Reverend and his wife got to work cleaning it up and making it their own when they made a horrible discovery. The reverend's wife was cleaning out a cupboard when she found a package wrapped in brown paper. When she unwrapped it, she found it contained the skull of a young woman.

After that, manifestations reached full-force. Vague shapes stalked the halls, lights turned on and off, pebbles appeared to fling themselves at the residents from out of nowhere, the phantom carriage drove past on the adjoining road, and the servants' bells began to ring. The bells, which all respectable homes had a hundred years ago, were located in the servants' quarters and attached to pull-ropes leading to each room of the house. Thus, if one of the residents wanted help in the drawing room, he could pull the rope and in the servants' quarters, a bell under a sign saying "Drawing Room" would ring. These bells started to go off at odd hours, even though the system had been disconnected in favor of a modern electric bell system. Even stranger, when the room of origin was investigated, nothing was ever found.

The new reverend also heard many moans and whispers. One of them said the phrase, "Don't, Carlos, don't." Later inquiries revealed that Carlos was the second Reverend Bull's nickname.

That year, the Smiths decided to contact British newspaper, the *Daily Mirror,* about their experiences. The paper sent a reporter and also called in a paranormal researcher named Harry Price. Many researchers wished the Smiths had never taken that step, because the involvement of the press and Mr. Price would only serve to muddy the waters around the events at Borley Rectory.

A picture alleging to depict one of the ghosts at the rectory

Harry Price was the best-known paranormal investigator of his generation. Although still in the early years of his career, he had been involved in numerous cases and was already well-known to the press and public. What was less known to those outside his inner circle was that he was an accomplished magician who had been practicing conjuring tricks and slights of hand since his childhood, and who had made his living on the stage for a time. Many later investigators pointed out that having a man adept at conjuring fake magical phenomena investigating supposedly real magical phenomena was a reasonable cause for suspicion. Several paranormal investigators flatly accused Price of making up many of the supposed happenings, although as many residents and visitors had reported paranormal activity, it can't be said that he made the hauntings up on his own.

Price

When Price made the first of many visits to Borley Rectory on June 12, he stopped to ask a local for directions. The man replied, "Oh, you mean the most haunted house in England." That phrase would soon make it into the headlines and was adopted as the title of Price's first book on the rectory. His initial visit became a red-letter day in the history of Borley Rectory, with a number of strange occurrences never before witnessed in the home. Objects such as stones and vases flew across the room, and Price had a conversation with a spirit that tapped out messages on a picture frame. When Price left at the end of the day, the manifestations stopped. Smith's wife later went on record saying she thought Price had done the tricks himself, but the genie was nevertheless out of the bottle.

Now that the press was interested, more reporters arrived at the home, and Harry Price returned, wanting to continue his investigations. There was a frenzy of breathless reporting of ghosts and restless spirits at what hack reporters eagerly advertised as "the most haunted house in England."

The Smiths left the following month, relieved to be rid of both the ghosts and the reporters, and the rectory stood empty for nearly a year while the parish scrambled to find someone willing to live in it. Finally, in 1930, the Reverend Lionel Algernon Foyster, his wife Marianne, and their young daughter, Adelaide, moved in, only to discover that the ghosts hadn't moved out. The family was plagued by various poltergeist phenomena, such as the ringing of the servants' bells, rocks breaking windows and flying around the room, and Marianne being thrown from her bed by an unseen assailant. Poor little Adelaide was even locked in a room when there was no key with which to lock the door.

The reverend tried to perform an exorcism, but he was hit by a flying rock that interrupted his ritual. A second attempt proved equally fruitless - the ghosts at Borley Rectory weren't going anywhere.

The strange story of the house took a new turn when writing began to appear on the walls. One witness saw a pencil rise from a desk as if lifted by an unseen hand and start writing on a wall. The messages would always be an almost illegible scribble, a desperate scrawl that wrote over itself. Some could not be deciphered. Others showed the name Marianne fairly clearly. Sometimes they said short phrases such as "Marianne, Rest," "Marianne help me," and "Marianne say mass prayers." Another appeared to read, "Marianne, please help me get out."

These notes were directed at Marianne Foyster, who appeared to be at the center of this particular phenomenon. The reverend's wife even tried to have conversations with the spirit, encouraging it to write on a piece of paper. When the scribbles appeared, she would try to figure out what they said and respond back. This method of communication eventually failed because the writing was too messy. It should be noted that many of the scribblings were written on the walls at the height of an adult and thus could not have been written by Adelaide, who was still a toddler.

One exchange between Marianne and the spirit written on the hallway leading to the bathroom was recorded by Lionel Foyster in a diary he kept. The entry for June 30, 1931, reads, "'Marianne' appeared one day on the wall of the passage leading down to the bathroom. It looked as if the writer had been pulled away just as he was finishing, since the end of the 'e' went up in the air and the 'i' was not dotted. I wrote underneath, 'What can we do?', but no notice was taken of it. Later, a little further along the passage, was written, 'Marianne please help get,' and then a dash as if, again, someone had been pulled away. Later still, further along the passage, was written, 'Marianne get help (something undecipherable) bother me' (or bothers me). Marianne wrote underneath, 'I cannot understand, tell me more. Marianne.' Something was added underneath but subsequently written over."

The spirit writings are one of the most controversial aspects of the Borley Rectory story. Many accused Marianne of writing them herself, and when the writings were analyzed by a graphologist, he said that the scribblings and Marianne's responses were written by the same hand, although the spirit scrawlings were so messy that one must wonder how they could have analyzed them at all. Marianne's son strongly denied that the spirit messages were in the same handwriting as his mother's. Harry Price himself, although a firm believer in ghosts, thought Marianne might have been responsible. Both he and other investigators thought that while the messages might have been written by her, they could have been done in a form of "automatic writing" in which a spirit takes over the hand of a subject and uses it to write its own communications.

The Foysters moved out in October of 1935, the Reverend explaining that he suffered from declining health and was no longer able to perform his duties. Many locals whispered that the ghosts had chased them out, or that the reverend's ill health was due to the stress of having to constantly deal with menacing manifestations of the unknown.

Once again, the house remained vacant as the church scrambled to find a clergyman willing to take on the challenge of living there. Price, the paranormal investigator, saw it as a chance to further his studies and rented the house for a year in May of 1937. He stayed there himself at times, but he also hired 48 part-time assistants to stay there on other nights to take notes on anything they experienced that might be considered out of the ordinary.

Oddly, the ghosts were quiet during this period. They had come out more strongly around Marianne, and once she had departed, they subsided into the background. Occasionally, the volunteers heard footsteps or found that objects had moved from their places, but little else was reported. Many noted that some parts of the rectory were noticeably and inexplicably colder than the other rooms.

One of Price's assistants, Helen Glanville, held a séance concerning the house on October 31, 1937. She wasn't actually at Borley Rectory at the time, but rather, in London. Perhaps she felt a séance in the rectory itself would be too dangerous. During her séance, she made contact with two spirits, one of them the nun several people had seen stalking the grounds. The spirit had said her name was Marie Lairre. She'd said that as a young woman, she had run away from her nunnery in France in order to move to Borley and marry the love of her life, a member of the local nobility called Henry Waldegrave. Historical records show there was, indeed, a noble family of that name in the area in the 17th century. Marie said she had been cruelly murdered by being thrown down a well. Could it have been the spirit of Marie Lairre who had written "Marianne, please help me get out" on the wall?

The second spirit that contacted Helen Glanville through her séance had called himself Sunex Amures, and he gave a dire warning that he would burn the house down at 9:00 p.m. on the night of March 27, 1938. He promised that when the house burned down, the bones of a murder victim would be revealed.

As it turned out, Sunex Amures did not burn the house down—its new owner did. On February 27, 1939, Captain W. H. Gregson was stocking some bookshelves in his new home when he accidentally knocked an oil lamp over. The flames spread too quickly for Gregson to stop them, and he had to flee. The house went up in a sheet of flame and burned for eight hours, defying the efforts of the local fire services. When it was all over, the house had been gutted, the walls left barely standing, the roof caved in, and everything inside had burnt to cinders.

For many years, the ruins stood as a somber testament to the terror that had gripped the small Essex town. Price went back again in August 1943, remembering the spirit's promise that a murder victim would be found in the ruins. He dug and discovered two bones he said were from a young woman. Some locals cried foul, saying the bones were actually from a pig. When Price tried to get them buried in the Borley churchyard, county officials refused. Eventually, he arranged for them to have a Christian burial in another cemetery.

The next year, the ruins were finally pulled down.

As one grim final chapter to the tale of the house, a widely published photograph shows the rectory in ruins, but viewers can clearly see a brick hovering in the air above the rubble.

Harry Price, who had popularized the hauntings more than anyone else, died in 1948, having spent almost 20 years investigating the case and writing extensively on it. His two books on the Borley Rectory were bestsellers, and at the time of his death, he was busy working on a third. While already a leading figure in the occult field when he started his investigations, it would not be an exaggeration to say that the Borley Rectory had made his career. Both of his books are still sought out by those interested in this remarkable case of haunting and poltergeist activity.

The destruction of the Borley Rectory did not stop the hauntings. The nun was seen in the nearby Borley Church churchyard, the origins of which are lost to history. There was most probably a wooden church there at the time of the Norman Conquest in 1066, and we do know a stone church was built in the 12th century. Like most early churches in England, it has since been expanded and renovated many times, most notably in the 14th and 15th and 16th centuries, but traces of the original medieval structure can still be seen.

The Reverend Alfred Clifford Henning, rector of the combined parishes of Borley and Liston until his death in 1955, reported hearing the organ playing at night and the sound of footsteps when he was alone inside of the locked church. Some of these incidents happened before the destruction of Borley Rectory, so it appears there has always been some restless spirits at work in the holy building. However, sightings became more frequent once the rectory had burned down. Whether this is a case of the ghosts moving house or simply because investigators paid more attention to the church is not clear.

One early occurrence was reported by the Reverend Harry Bull, who was with a friend in the church one day when they heard a strange tapping noise outside. The taps grew louder, sounding as if they had entered the church. The tapping then moved about the walls before finally going silent. The two baffled men explored both the outside and inside of the church and could find no obvious source for the noise.

Several visitors to Borley Church have also experienced overpowering, unpleasant smells. In one case from 1949, Susanna Dudley of Newmarket and her three friends visited the church grounds one windy February day when they were almost knocked out by a powerful stench. Dudley thought it had smelled like embalming fluid, while the others thought it had smelled like heavy incense. The smell persisted in a localized area of only a few yards in diameter for quite some time, despite the strong wind that day. Modern witnesses have heard ghostly chanting coming from within the locked church at night. The phantom nun has appeared many times in the churchyard, once even looking quite solid in the broad daylight before vanishing into thin air.

The most intriguing events occurred during an investigation by the Enfield Paranormal Research Group in 1970, led by Geoffrey Croom-Hollingsworth and Roy Potter. Their results were made into a BBC documentary called *The Ghost Hunters* in 1975. The group spent several nights in the churchyard and inside the church itself, keeping watch. They brought with them a series of tape recorders in order to capture any strange sounds that might occur.

The team got more than they bargained for when the tapes captured loud bangs, light rapping noises, deep thuds, and footsteps. While these could have been made by the investigators themselves even as they took care to keep quiet and stay still, the tapes also recorded the sound of doors opening when the church was all locked up. There were also a number of frightening sighs and groans. When the BBC accompanied them on one of their nights in the church, the camera crew set up some distance away from the three paranormal investigators, who sat in one of the pews. Late in the night, the church suddenly grew much colder and little pinpricks of light appeared in the air, slowly approaching the three investigators before vanishing. At that same moment, there was a loud crash as if some unseen object had been thrown onto the stone floor.

Even today, more than 70 years after the rectory ruins have been swept away, psychics and paranormal investigators still make pilgrimages to the site in an effort to pick up on vibrations from beyond. Some firmly believe that not all of the spirits have left the site of what was once known as the "Most Haunted House in England."

The Most Haunted House in London

THE "HAUNTED HOUSE," BERKELEY SQUARE.

While the controversy continues over whether the Borley Rectory was or was not haunted, another home has taken on the mantle of the "Most Haunted House in London." Number 50 Berkeley Square is an unassuming Late Georgian period townhouse in London's high-end neighborhood of Mayfair. Berkeley Square certainly doesn't look like the typical place for a haunting—it's a beautiful square set away from the hustle and bustle of London's busier financial and shopping districts. Here, there are homes and quieter offices for various financial companies. Laid out in the middle of the 18th century, it has a fine garden that, unlike many others in London's finer districts, is open to the public. One can relax on the grass and admire the tall Plane trees, planted shortly after the square had been laid out.

It appears that trouble first began at the house in the late 19th century after a hundred years of peace. Perhaps no one had yet died in the house who wished to stay on this Earth. The restless spirit may be one of the famous former residents. Prime Minister George Canning lived there until his death in 1827. While he was, by far, the most famous person to have owned the house, the other owners tended to be important figures of the day in their own right.

Canning

In 1859, a Mr. Myers moved in. It was then that the hauntings began, or at least, the first manifestations to be recorded for posterity. This was already the scientific age and many people no longer believed in ghosts. To report one tended to invite ridicule.

Mr. Myers reported plenty of ghosts and things started to go badly for him in a very mundane way. He was engaged to be married and spent a large amount of money fitting out the house to his fiancé's expectations only for her to jilt him at the last minute. Falling into a deep depression, Myers became a recluse. He no longer maintained his house, saw no one, and lived only in a small servants quarters on the top floor. He would never answer the door except when a servant, who did not live at the property, came to bring him food. Neighbors could sometimes see Myers wandering the house at night, lighting his way with a single candle. Occasionally, they heard strange sounds and babbling emanating from the lonely home. Myers never stepped outside, and what little details his neighbors could glean from the servant indicated that he had gone mad. The property gradually fell into decay—the windows were never washed, the soot was never scrubbed from the walls, and what could be seen of the interior through the windows looked tattered and covered with dust.

Rumors began to circulate that Myers wasn't the only being wandering the house at night.

When he was brought to court in 1873 for failure to pay his council tax, the magistrate let him off due to the fact that he had lived in "the haunted house," an unusual way to dodge taxes if ever there was one. He died the next year, with his taxes still unpaid.

Later residents of the house reported that the hauntings were centered around the same room in which Myers had lived, but strangely, most stories said it was not the spirit of the jilted bachelor who had been causing the trouble. The attic room where Myers had spent his lonely vigil mourning his love life was apparently the scene of a suicide. Sometime before Myers had moved in, a young women supposedly hanged herself there after having been molested by her uncle. She is said to appear as a ghostly white figure or occasionally a brown mist. A variant of the tale says it was of a young girl who had been killed by her servant.

Either way, the ghost was a terrifying one that was ultimately responsible for killing more than one witness. In 1879, *Mayfair Magazine* reported that a maid who didn't know the story of the haunted room had taken up residence there. One night, ear-splitting screams rang through the house. When the owners ran up to the servant's quarters to investigate, they found the maid in a frenzy, babbling about having seen a ghost. She could not be calmed down and was sent to an asylum, where she died of heart failure the next day, literally scared to death.

By this time, the upstairs room had developed quite a reputation. George William Lyttelton, the 4th Baron Lyttelton, offered to stay in the haunted room. Unlike many people who had boasted they weren't afraid of haunted houses and offered to stay in them overnight, Lyttelton was not a doubter. He stayed in the room not to disprove the ghost, but to prove his own bravery, strengthening his courage by bringing his trusty shotgun along. Around the middle of the night, the ghostly girl appeared. In shock, Lyttelton fired at it, proving chivalry is dead when it came to the dead.

A contemporary sketch depicting Lyttelton

The next day, Lyttelton investigated the attic with the aid of daylight but could find no trace of the ghost. He was sure he had hit it since he had fired with a shotgun at point-blank range, but there was no trace of blood, only the scattering of the shot on the opposite wall. Whatever he had seen that night, it had been no human hoaxer.

Had the house been haunted before Myers had become a recluse? In his depression, had he gained some sick satisfaction sleeping in a haunted room and keeping company with a ghost who was just as unhappy as he was? Did his own disinterest in life give him immunity to the terror of seeing the ghost? Whatever the truth of the tale, both Myers and the ghost have moved on, and there haven't been any reported hauntings at 50 Berkeley Square for a couple of generations.

Haunted Churches in England

Borley Church is far from the only house of worship said to be home to restless spirits. Another Essex church, a mere 20 miles south of Borley, has been called the "Most Haunted Church in England."

St. Andrew's Church stood in the village of Langenhoe near the town of Colchester. Situated on a low rise above marshlands a few miles from the sea, there is little to the village of Langenhoe, even today. Despite its population being fewer than 600, a church was first built there in the 14th century. It was badly damaged in a rare English earthquake in 1884. The structure was repaired but slowly deteriorated thereafter, and it was eventually declared unstable and torn down in 1962.

For many years before its demolition, strange tales were inspired by Langenhoe Church and its associated buildings, including reports of a "Lady in Black," seen in the church at night. In 1908, two sisters saw the ghostly figure of a nun in the graveyard. The nun glided between the gravestones until she reached the north wall near the western end of the church, passed right through the wall, and disappeared.

Matters grew worse when a new rector arrived at Langenhoe in 1937. The Reverend Ernest Merryweather did not believe in ghosts and arrived thinking he was taking on a routine job in service of the church. He was soon proven wrong on both counts.

The sightings began rather unobtrusively, the first incident being when Merryweather found that his valise, which he had left in the vestry, had somehow locked itself. Try as he might, he couldn't get it open. Frustrated, he finally left for the day. To his astonishment, when he tried to reopen the valise at home, he had no trouble. This odd occurrence happened several times, though he discovered that he was always able to open the valise as soon as he had left the church.

More events soon followed, piquing the Reverend's curiosity enough to keep a journal of them. The entry for September 20, 1937 records that it had been a quiet day with no wind, but when he was inside the church, the heavy, old, wooden door suddenly slammed shut with enough force to shake the stone building. He often found objects had moved when no one else was inside the church, and he heard thuds coming from the vestry.

The strange events ended as mysteriously as they had begun. For a time, Merryweather had forgotten about the spirits, at least until they came back in 1950 even stronger than before. The rector's diary for September 28, 1950 notes that while he was in the vestry, he heard a young woman chanting plainsong in the nave at the western end of the church. Then, he heard the slow sound of footsteps coming up the aisle. Curious, he crept out of the vestry hoping to catch whoever was in the church, but as soon as he had gone through the door, all of the sounds stopped and there was no one to be seen.

The phantom singer returned sometime later that year, when she was heard by the rector and two workmen. The workmen had been doing a job on the grounds when they heard singing coming from the locked and empty building. Merryweather arrived to find the workmen peeking through a keyhole, trying to catch a glimpse of the mysterious singer. He opened the church, but even though they searched the entire building, they found no one.

An even stranger occurrence happened later that same year. On the night of Christmas Eve, Merryweather was walking up the nave when he saw a dark figure pass before him. Though it was difficult to make out, it had looked like a man dressed in a tweed suit. The figure went to the pulpit and then disappeared.

The rector saw even more figures. Once, while practicing on the church organ, he had the feeling someone was standing behind him. He turned around and caught a brief glimpse of a woman in modern clothing before she vanished into thin air. Several times while standing at the altar, helping with Sunday services, Merryweather spotted a woman wearing Tudor-era clothing pass along the western end of the church behind the parishioners and walk right through a wall.

What was unusual about many of these experiences—some of the figures, and the ghostly organ music heard by the workmen—was that they had occurred during the daytime.

By that time, the damage that had been caused to the church in the great Colchester Earthquake of 1884 had undone all repairs, and the church closed to services in 1955. The Reverend Merryweather no doubt breathed a sigh of relief that he no longer had to deal with the many spirits at the church. He retired in 1959 and died in 1965, three years after the old haunted church was demolished.

Nothing remains of Langenhoe Church today, except for the overgrown graveyard. It is a lonely place, quiet and unattended. Ghosthunters who seek it out say they feel an ominous dread about the place, as if whatever malefic force had once terrorized the church still lingers in the graveyard, 50 years after the church was torn down.

Borley Church is also far from the only house of worship visited by a spectral nun. The tale of a nun falling in love with a priest, monk, or member of the laity is told in many locations. The tale usually involves a man and a nun wanting to run off together, but getting caught and being either beheaded or bricked up in a wall. One such story is associated with Chicksands Priory in Clophill, Bedfordshire. Established in 1150, it is noteworthy for having the only surviving cloister of the Gilbertine Order. It was also unusual in that both monks and nuns lived there, albeit in separate buildings. While the exact layout of the original priory is unclear, the monks and nuns probably had cells around their own separate cloisters, divided by the church.

At the priory's height, the residents numbered about a hundred. When King Henry VIII took it over for himself during the Dissolution of the Monasteries, he gave the residents pensions and cottages in which to spend the rest of their days, a better deal than he had given most monastic orders, since the Gilbertines hadn't caused him any trouble. The king dissolved the priory on October 22, 1538. The Gilbertines, having no other priories at the time, thus ceased to exist. The priory passed into the hands of the noble Snowe family and then the Osborn family, until the government purchased it in 1936. From 1940-1995 it served as a base for the Royal Air Force and the United States Air Force.

Henry VIII

The legend of the fallen nun at Chicksands Priory is similar to other such tales, in which a nun named Berta Rosata and a canon whose name has been lost to history supposedly fell in love and began meeting in secret after dark. The nun got pregnant, as nuns generally do in these stories, and when her condition began to show, she was tortured until she confessed. The church elders sentenced her and the canon to death. The nun was put into a niche and bricked up until only a small slit remained for her to see through so she could witness her lover get beheaded. Once that grisly task had been accomplished, the remaining bricks were put in place and the nun either suffocated or starved.

The execution was on the 17th of the month. Local legend says that on the 17th of every month since that fateful day, the nun can be seen walking the grounds of the priory, looking for her dead lover.

Locals point to a plaque over the eastern wall of the surviving cloister as having been placed in memory to the dead nun. It readsm "By virtues guarded and by manners graced, Here alas is fair Rosata placed." Historians dismiss this plaque, saying the style dates it to the late 18th century, a time when Gothic tales were all the rage and a story about a bricked-up, pregnant nun would have had wide appeal. In addition, a historical linguist stated that there is no record of the name Rosata being used in the Middle Ages. Furthermore, the wording of the plaque does not correspond to the story.

A historical note from 1534 does, however, give some credence to the tale. In that year, Dr. Richard Layton visited the priory, writing to Oliver Cromwell that he had found "two of the said nunnes not baron [barren]." One had been impregnated by a superior, the other by a male servant.

Whatever truth to the tale of the seduced nun there might be, there do seem to be restless spirits in Chicksands Priory. In the King James Room, which serves as a picture gallery, a woman dressed in black has been seen gliding across the floor and disappearing into a wall. She is said to have long hair that covers her face, so this could not be the nun, unless the image is so vague that a nun's habit has been mistaken for hair. A female staff member working in the same room saw a woman in what looked like a wedding dress with a long white train pass by her and into a wall. What is interesting about this sighting is that the startled witness was able to hear the rustling of the dress as she moved past. Most ghost sightings are not accompanied by sounds. Noises tend to be the signature of poltergeists, and those particular spirits rarely show themselves.

During the time the United States Air Force was in residence, the troops experienced a couple of strange events. In August of 1954, a flight lieutenant awoke at 3:45 in the morning, deciding to read for a bit before falling back to sleep, but when he switched on the light, he was shocked to see "there at the side of my bed a woman with a ruddy face and untidy hair, wearing a dark dress with a white lace collar. She appeared to be holding a notepad. She moved to the foot of my bed and vanished."

In March of 1957, another officer was admiring the pictures in the King James Room when he saw the image of a "motionless head and shoulders of a middle-aged woman dressed in what we associate with a nun's head-dress. She was looking past me with an expression of serious thought."

It is strange that of these and the many other sightings at the priory, so few of them seem to involve a nun.

Chicksands Priory is no longer a military base and is now open to visitors, more than one of whom has seen something strange pass through the picture gallery.

Embarrassed nuns aren't the only spirits who haunt churches. In St. John's Church in Torquay, Devonshire, it was an irate organist. This is a rare case in which people actually know the name of the spirit, and not as some shadowy figure in a folktale but as a person proven to have actually existed. Henry Ditton-Newman played the organ at the church for many years and grew very popular for his expert ability. He even composed his own music. One of his collections of compositions, *Hymn-Tunes and other Music*, was published after he died on November 19, 1883.

His passing was a grievous loss to the congregation, but old Henry didn't fully leave. Soon he reappeared, glimpsed standing near the organ he had once played so well. The Reverend Hitchcock and several parishioners had seen him on and off for a few years before his ghost had finally faded away. Some said that Henry was composing some music when he died, and he was hovering close to the organ in order to finish it. Perhaps, they said, he had finished his composition and was playing it on the other side, which is why he no longer visited his old church.

Then, in 1956, Henry came back. The organist at the time was frightened one Sunday when he saw a dark figure in old-fashioned clothing appear at his side as he was playing. The ghost returned the next Sunday and the Sunday after that, until the organist refused to play in the church any longer.

Later that year, the Reverend Rouse, in charge of the church at the time, decided to replace Henry's old organ, having claimed it had worn out, rather than that it was because of a spirit attached to it. Be that as it may, after the new organ was installed, Henry Ditton-Newman was never seen in St. John's Church again.

Haunted Ruins in England

England is a historic land, and in the countryside and smaller villages, many storied ruins stand as mute testimony to the past. Not all of their former residents realize their days are over, however. One such case is Minster Lovell Hall, a 15th-century manor house that stands along the

River Windrush in the lovely Oxfordshire countryside.

John Salmon's picture of the ruins of Minster Lovell Hall

There has been a manor on that site for more than a thousand years. One is listed in the *Domesday Book* of 1086, when it had 29 households and two mills. King Henry I (1100-1135) granted the land to a baron named William, whom his friends had nicknamed "Lupellus" or "Lone Wolf." This later changed to "Lovell," becoming the family name and the name of the manor itself. The structure standing today was built by the 7th Baron William Lovell in the 1940s (died 1455). It remained in the family until the defeat of the Yorkists in the War of the Roses. The Lovells, being Yorkists, had all of their lands seized by the Crown in 1485.

Lord Francis Lovell was one of the main supporters of the Yorkist faction that had backed King Richard III's claim to the throne. The king had even visited Minster Lovell to spend time with one of his favorite followers. When the war turned against them, the king and Lovell fled to Flanders in 1485.

Two years later, Lovell was back, this time supporting an Oxfordshire youth named Lambert Simnel as king, gathering many of his old Yorkist allies, and marching through Lancashire and the Midlands to Stoke near Newark, where they met the eventual Tudor king, Henry VII, in battle. The Yorkists were decisively defeated, and Lovell was claimed to have drowned as he tried to swim his horse across the River Trent in an effort to get away.

However, a local rumor says he escaped and fled back to his beloved Minster Lovell Hall where he lived in a hidden room, being fed by a loyal servant. Some say the room was a hidden crypt beneath Minster Lovell Hall, although no such chamber is known today. The arrangement went on for years until the servant died suddenly and Lovell, having no way to get out, starved to death. Generations later, in 1708, when alterations were being made to the manor, workmen came upon the secret chamber and were amazed to see the well-preserved body of a man sitting at a desk with a pen, paper, and books arranged before him. According to the report, no sooner had the fresh air rushed into the formerly sealed chamber "than the figure collapsed, and when the spectators ran to inspect the mystery all that remained was the rich dress of a noble, and the dust of Lord Lovell's body."

Minster Lovell Hall remained a Crown property until 1602, when it was given to the Coke family. The Cokes lived there until 1747, when they moved to a new mansion at Holkham Hall, partially dismantling Minster Lovell to reuse the stone for their new home.

Now, the Minster stands as a hollowed-out ruin, but a picturesque one that has become popular with hikers and picnicking families. The general layout is still clearly visible, with the Minster taking up three sides of a large courtyard and the more humble buildings—such as the stable and kitchen—on one side, the hall and chapel on another, and the west wing that had been given over to living quarters, a common layout in late medieval manor houses. But when the day-trippers leave and the sun sets, it's said the Minster's old owner comes back. Groans, footsteps, and the rustling of papers are heard issuing from the earth, and the occasional figure of a tall man wearing a cloak is seen walking the grounds. Since these sightings are rare, it might mean that the last of the Lovells has finally found some peace.

A more romantic story, called "The Tale of the Mistletoe Bough," is still told by the old folks of Oxfordshire. They say that during the final years of the Lovell residence at the Minster, there was a grand celebration to honor one of the Lovell daughters having been betrothed to her childhood sweetheart. It took place around Christmastime, when the mistletoe berries were on the bough.

Late in the evening, as the older folks sat half slumbering in their seats from having drunk too much mead and beer, the younger guests decided to play a game of hide and seek. Someone was named "it" and the rest of the assembly ran off to remote chambers and attic rooms to find the best place to hide. Of course, the bride had a distinct advantage, having grown up playing Hide and Seek in that very house. Lifting up the hem of her wedding dress so she could make better time, she hurried away from the warm and well-lit rooms and up to the attic, used to store lumber and other items not regularly in use. She knew there was a large, heavy-lidded oak chest up there that happened to be empty, and no one would think to look for her in there. She opened the lid with some difficulty and climbed inside, closing it behind her.

The person who had been declared "it" had found every one of the hiding places, save one. Where had the bride gone? The alarm was raised and guests and servants fanned out to search every inch of the manor with no luck. The search continued for days, spreading out to the nearby fields and forest, but they couldn't find a trace of her. In the end, everyone had decided that young woman must have had second thoughts and fled with another lover. Distraught, the groom rode sadly away. Later, he made a suicidal charge against some knights of the Lancastrian faction and died at their hands.

Many years later, while some workmen were clearing out the dusty old attic, they came across the chest. It was old and eaten through by worms, and the new owners of the house ordered it to be thrown away, but when the workmen tried to lift it, the chest collapsed into pieces and a skeleton fell to the floor. It was dressed in a once-fine wedding dress, now as worm-eaten and faded as the chest. On the boney fingers were several gold rings, including a wedding ring, and one that bore the Lovell family seal.

It was then the locals had remembered the disappearance of the Lovell bride from several generations before. Apparently, when the young woman had closed the top of the chest over her, the latch had snapped shut and she had been unable to lift the lid up again. The chest was so thick that her screams for help went unheard. Perhaps, late at night, she still tries to scream, hoping to be discovered and reunited with her lover at last.

An even more ancient place that might house ghosts is England's most impressive stone circle - not Stonehenge, but Avebury. 17 miles north of the famous stone circle is the little village of Avebury, the site of England's most extensive set of megalithic monuments.

Ethan Doyle White's picture of part of the Avebury henge

Avebury is a massive stone circle more than a thousand feet in diameter, surrounded by a deep ditch and earthen rampart thirty feet high. Some of the stones are huge, weighing as much as 40 tons. Two smaller stone circles stand inside the larger one. An avenue flanked by standing stones heads south to a smaller stone circle. There used to be another one heading west, but it has mostly disappeared. Prehistoric Britons started erecting this incredible monument around 3000 BC.

John Aubrey, the first antiquarian to have investigated the site, wrote in the 17th century that Avebury "does as much exceed in greatness the so renowned Stonehenge, as a cathedral doeth a parish church."

The megalithic complex at Avebury is remarkably well-preserved despite its age and the number of people over the years that have wanted to do damage to it due to religious intolerance, greed, or simple neglect. During the Middle Ages, the local priests started a religious revival, whipping up anger against the Pagan monument and whole villages marched out to destroy the stones. They stacked kindling and logs soaked with pitch against the walls to start bonfires whose heat cracked the great stones apart. The villagers then hauled the pieces away for use in local buildings.

Aubrey

The vandalism didn't all go the way the villagers had planned. An enduring local tale relates how a group of men tried to topple one of the larger stones which fell over the wrong way, crushing one of them to death. For many years, this was dismissed as nothing more than local folklore since no one was able to name the man who had been killed or even in which century it was supposed to have happened, but in 1938, archaeologists dug up a fallen stone with the shattered skeleton of a man beneath it. With him were some coins dating to the 14th century. Even more intriguing, he also had on him the tools of a barber-surgeon. Back in those days, barbers often doubled as folk healers and were considered to have knowledge of magical cures. The villagers had apparently thought it would have been best to have someone with a knowledge of magic along, since the stone circle itself was considered magical. When the megalith's magic had won, the barber-surgeon's death became enshrined in local folk memory. The stone he helped topple has now been placed back upright to stand proud and defiant. It has since been dubbed "the Barber Stone."

Besides evidence of medieval work accidents, other mysteries surround Avebury. Two narrow escapes are recorded in local folklore. In one, a cobbler who had been working beneath one of the stones on a Sunday—an act prohibited by the Church—got up to continue his journey when he heard a loud crash. He turned around to find the stone he had been sitting under only a moment before had fallen over and he surely would have been crushed to death if he hadn't gotten up.

In another incident, a parish clerk was caught out on Salisbury Plain during a thunderstorm. He sought shelter under one of the stones for a time but decided it would be best to make his way home. He hadn't taken many steps away from the stone when a bolt of lightning blew it apart.

Residents of the tiny village of Avebury, nestled within the megalithic monument itself, tell of strange occurrences in the stone circle at night after the visitors leave, when shadowy figures flit between the stones and eerie chanting rises from the fields and stone circles. Nor are the hauntings confined to the ancient ruins. The local pub, The Red Lion, has the double distinction of being the only pub in Britain to be surrounded by a stone circle and be voted one of the top 10 most haunted bars in the world. The pub has quite a bit of history. It started as a farmhouse in the early 17th century before becoming a coaching inn in 1802, acting as a rest stop for the growing network of horse-drawn coaches taking passengers and mail between cities. It continues to serve drinks to this day.

The Red Lion's landlord says there are at least five ghosts in his pub. The best known is a young woman named Florrie, who married a local soldier in the 17th century. When he went off to fight in the English Civil War, she took another lover. The soldier returned unexpectedly, discovered them together, and shot the man who had cuckolded him before stabbing Florrie and throwing her down a well located inside the building. The well is still there today, and she is often seen hovering nearby or floating in and out of it. Sometimes, she is not seen, but acts as a poltergeist, throwing small objects across the bar.

Florrie seems to be attracted to men with beards. Locals suspect either her lover or her husband had worn one because she mostly appears to bearded men. Once, a fellow with a beard walked into the pub and guests were startled to see the chandelier spin around like a top as he passed beneath it.

In typical English humor, the landlord covered the well with glass and made it into a table for his drinkers. Out of respect for Florrie, he put a brass plaque on it to commemorate her murder.

Two spectral children have also been seen, as well as a woman who may be their deceased mother. All three apparitions are usually seen in one of the bedrooms. When seen together, the two children huddle in a corner trembling with fright, while the woman stands nearby, ignoring them.

Another restless resident is that of a former owner, supposedly murdered in the 17th century. The story goes that he had hidden some outlaws in the cellar, but they double-crossed and murdered him. He can now be seen, knife in hand, searching for the outlaws in order to get his vengeance.

Other witnesses have seen a ghostly coach and four horses pull up in front of the pub, its driver still thinking the pub is open for business as a coaching inn. More often, only the hooves are heard clopping in the courtyard outside. This usually happens late at night, and the staff never go out to investigate. The rumor is that the horses are harbingers of evil, and no one wants to tempt fate.

Avebury is set within an ancient landscape of monuments, such as prehistoric burial mounds, rock carvings, and ancient earthworks. The entire area has been designated a World Heritage Site. The most visited and impressive site besides the Stonehenge and Avebury is the West Kennet Long Barrow, which stands atop a ridge, only a short walk from Avebury. The West Kennet Long Barrow is one of the largest Neolithic tombs in Britain. Built around 3650 BCE, it was the final resting place for about 50 people. It consists of a long chamber of stones covered with earth. Interestingly, the entrance was reopened several times in antiquity in order to place new burials inside. Judging from the style of artifacts, the last burial was around 2600 BC, meaning the tomb had been in use for about a thousand years. The entire long barrow measures 328 feet long (100 meters), 82 feet wide (25 meters) at its widest point, and 10.5 feet high (3.2 meters). Originally, it had bare chalk sides that gleamed in the sun, making it visible for miles around. After it had been finally sealed, the entire structure was covered with turf.

A picture of part of the West Kennet Long Barrow

Like Avebury, the barrow has suffered vandalism in more recent centuries. In the 1600s, a certain Dr. Troope of Marlborough broke into the tomb to retrieve some of the bones in order to brew up a "noble medicine that relieved my distressed neighbours [sic]."

The barrow is haunted by several ghosts, the most frequently seen of which appears just before dawn on the summer solstice. Local farmers tell of seeing a man dressed in white robes, standing at the barrow's eastern end with a powerfully built dog with bright red ears at his side. Both figures stand stock still, waiting for first light. As soon as the sun rises above the horizon, the two turn and enter the barrow.

Other ghosts are felt, rather than seen, and some visitors are overcome by an oppressive sense of dread. One woman who had visited in 1992 felt unseen hands grab her and try to pull her into the deepest part of the barrow. She fought to make it back to the entrance, feeling a heavy weight pressing down on her which slowed her movements. She finally broke free and into the daylight, having never seen who or what had attacked her.

Haunted Castles in England

The fortifications of the Middle Ages are some of England's best-loved landmarks. They are from various eras, some of them dating all the way back to Roman times, while hundreds had been made by the Norman conquerors after 1066. Every century saw new ones added, until after the English Civil War in the 17th century when many were dismantled so they couldn't be used as fortifications again.

One storied castle is Lympne Castle on the coast of Kent, which started its life as a Roman watchtower, a part of the Saxon Shore fortifications that had been built in the late 4th century to ward off Saxon pirates. After the Romans had left in 410 CE and the Angles, Saxons, and Jutes had moved in to start the Anglo-Saxon era, it lay unused for several centuries until a formidable castle was built on its foundations in 1360. For a time, it was owned by the Archdeacons of Canterbury; Thomas Beckett lived there for several years before becoming Archbishop.

A 19th century depiction of the castle

As is the case with many other English castles, Lympne Castle fell into disuse in the modern era. When it was purchased by Henry Beecham in 1905, he had a lot of restoration work to do. It wasn't until 1916 that he and his wife were able to move in. To their horror, they found the restorations had cleared out the bats, birds' nests, and loose stones, but it had not cleared out the ghosts.

The most common ghost is heard but never seen. Some nights, the heavy tread of booted feet is heard climbing the stairs of the old Roman watchtower, but is never heard coming down. The owners believe it to be the spirit of a Roman legionnaire, still on duty watching for Saxon pirates.

The other ghost is seen but never heard, that of a sad old priest standing in a small room in the western tower. The owner believes it might be one of seven bishops dispossessed and possibly murdered by Lanfranc, the first Norman Archbishop of Canterbury from 1070-1089, trusted councilor of William the Conqueror. Lanfranc got rid of many of the native English bishops and other high-ranking clergy to make way for his and William's personal favorites.

Lympne Castle has been extensively remodeled and now hosts weddings and corporate functions, though it is off-limits to the general public. An even more magnificent castle, one that can be visited, is Goodrich Castle in Herefordshire on the River Wye. Goodrich Castle is one of the most atmospheric fortifications in all of England. Most likely built by Godric of Mappestone shortly after the Norman invasion of England in 1066, it was originally a motte-and-bailey style castle, made up of an artificial hill with a wooden palisade and square, wooden keep atop it. At the foot of the artificial hill was another area enclosed with a wooden palisade. The entire fortification was surrounded by a ditch. These castles were quick, cheap to build, and proved difficult for the English, who lacked siege technology, to take. The Normans built them all over their newly conquered lands. Later generations strengthened the more important ones with stone walls and towers, turning them into proper castles.

Michael Eccles' picture of the ruins of Goodrich Castle

Such was the case with Goodrich Castle. In the 12th and 13th centuries, the castle was continuously expanded until it had become a large fortification with a great, square, stone keep, extensive living quarters, and formidable walls. It was an important defense on the Welsh border to assert dominance over the often-rebellious region, as it sat atop a rocky outcrop, overlooking a crossing of the River Wye on the border between England and Wales. As was the case with many other key fortifications, it was the scene of a bitter fight during the English Civil War.

It is during that siege that the ghost story begins. In 1646, the castle was held by the Royalist side when a Parliamentarian army led by Colonel John Birch marched against it. With him came his niece, Alice Birch. Though it may seem strange that a beautiful young woman would ride with an army into battle, the countryside was in chaos, and John Birch decided that the safest place for his ward was right by his side. Little did he know that he was leading her into more danger than he could possibly imagine.

Alice had a secret lover on the Royalist side, a dashing young soldier named Charles Clifford. As her uncle surrounded the castle, bombarding it with cannons and huge mortars capable of lobbing 200 pound balls over the walls, Alice waited for her chance to be reunited with Charles. Despite this formidable array of firepower, the stout walls of Goodrich Castle held out for some time, giving Alice the chance to pass a message through the opposing lines to her lover. They scheduled a rendezvous and under cover of darkness, she was able to slip past her uncle's sentries, enter the castle, and run into Clifford's arms.

This temporary happiness was cut short by the grim reality of war. John Birch and his Parliamentarian army were still outside, and the bombardment was beginning to take its toll. The water supply had been cut, many interior buildings had been wrecked, and the walls were beginning to crumble. The castle could not hold out much longer.

The young lovers decided to flee. Waiting for a dark and rainy night, Clifford mounted his trusty charger with Alice behind him and they galloped out of the castle. The Parliamentarian guards were so surprised by their sudden appearance that they didn't have time to stop them. Clifford led his steed down to the crossing on the River Wye, only to find the rain had swollen the river and the ford was impassable.

With John Birch's soldiers in hot pursuit, Clifford knew they must cross the river. He urged his steed onward. For a minute, it looked as if they'd make it, but then they reached the middle of the river, where the water was at its deepest and the current was at its swiftest, and the horse lost its footing and tumbled. Clifford and Alice fell into the water and were swept away, never to be seen again, at least not in this life. Now they are sometimes spotted on stormy nights, two terrified and soaked figures, clutching to the back of a ghostly horse as it tries to cross the river. At other times, the ill-fated lovers stand atop the ramparts, gazing forlornly across the river in the direction of the freedom they never enjoyed.

Haunted Graveyards across England

Tucked away in the little corners of historic London or in the yards of its finest churches, there are many old graveyards, each with stories to tell.

London's most famous burial ground, Highgate Cemetery, is renowned for its many famous permanent residents—such as Karl Marx and George Eliot—and for its elaborate nineteenth-century tombstones. Opened in 1839 to deal with a shortage of burial plots in the city, Highgate Cemetery is an atmospheric place that attracts many visitors for its peaceful greenery, its ornate statues of weeping angels, and its busts of prominent historical figures. In the cemetery, one can see foxes darting amidst the bushes and hear lively birdsong in the branches of shady trees.

Highgate Cemetery is one of London's larger historic cemeteries with more than 170,000 people buried and 53,000 graves. The disparity in numbers is due to the large number of family plots and crypts. Highgate was the most coveted spot in which to be buried during the Victorian era, but it had fallen into decline by the middle of the twentieth century, with vines overgrowing the tombstones and all sorts of undesirables breaking in at night. During the 1970s there was a vampire scare at the cemetery after several sacrificed animals and a headless, burnt corpse were found. Two competing occultists led groups through the cemetery at night, hunting for the supposed vampire. The whole story can be read in *The History and Folklore of Vampires: The Stories and Legends Behind the Mythical Beings* by Charles River Editors.

The cemetery has plenty of ghosts, too. One is of a disheveled old woman who runs this way and that amidst the gravestones as she desperately looks for her children, whom she murdered in a fit of madness. Recently, a man walking down adjoining Swains Lane at night was startled to see a dark figure pass right through the iron bars of the fence, swoop out onto the sidewalk, and knock him down. As the figure loomed over him, the pedestrian thought he was a dead man, but then a car passed down the road and when the light fell upon the dark figure, it vanished.

Another, quieter ghost is more frequently seen, that of a gray figure that appears to be a man, looking thoughtfully off into the distance. When approached, the figure silently fades away, only to reappear in another part of the cemetery. It was the sighting of the gray, ghostly figure that originally launched the first vampire investigations at Highgate, though the dead bodies appeared later, so the initial scare may have been a case of occultists mistaking a ghost for a vampire.

As strange as the case of the Highgate vampire and its associated ghosts may be, an even stranger one comes from a graveyard on Black Lion Lane in Hammersmith. Back in 1804, passersby noted a ghostly, white figure floating between the headstones. Sometimes, it rushed out of the graveyard to attack people. A local man named Francis Smith formed a vigilante committee and started to patrol the area at night. One evening, he was walking alone down Black Lion Lane when he saw an all-white figure walking toward him. Pulling out his trusty pistol, loaded and ready for the occasion, Smith shot the figure, but it turned out the figure was not the fearsome ghost, but a 22-year-old bricklayer. He hadn't been a ghost before the encounter, but Francis Smith had made one of him.

When hauled before the judge, Lord Chief Baron Macdonald, Smith pleaded innocence, saying that he had thought his life was in danger. At first, the jury was inclined to believe him and only find him guilty of manslaughter. Macdonald wasn't buying it, however, pointing out that Smith had been carrying a gun at that place and at that time with the specific intent to shoot anyone he came across that seemed suspicious. Macdonald convinced the jury to change the verdict to murder and promptly sentenced Smith to hang, thus creating two ghosts where there had once been none.

Luckily for Smith, he won the appeal, got the crime knocked back down to manslaughter, and ended up doing only one year of hard labor.

The Hammersmith ghost case went down in British legal history as an important ruling regarding the extent to which people are culpable for their actions when they think they are in danger.

Yes, England is so full of ghosts that one even made legal history.

Haunted Welsh Castles

Wales is a paradise for those who love castles; more than 600 castles have been built in the country, and more than a hundred of them are still standing. Tourism boosters claim that Wales has more castles per square mile than any other country in the world, a claim Belgium also makes. Since there's no independent, international body of castles-per-square-mile measurers, that argument will have to remain unresolved for now.

Regardless, there's no question that Wales has some spectacular castles to visit, and their crumbling walls and lofty towers are full of history, grisly tales of bloodletting, and allegedly more than a few restless spirits. A visit to one or more of these castles is well worth the excursion for the picturesque ruins, stunning views from atop the towers, and the chilling tales of what went on inside them.

The oldest fortification in Wales is not a castle but an earthwork. Offa's Dyke was built in the late 8th century CE by Offa, king of Mercia from 757-796, to act as a border defense between his kingdom and the Welsh kingdom of Powys on its western border.

Chris Heaton's pictures of parts of the dyke

While it looks rather unspectacular today, Offa's Dyke was a monumental undertaking. It consisted of a ditch 65 feet (20 m) wide and rampart 8 feet (2.4 m) high. The earthwork ran 150 miles (240 km) from Liverpool Bay south to the Severn Estuary, cutting Wales off from the rest of Britain. The modern border still roughly follows its route, as does a national trail, and the earthwork remains the focus of many archaeological excavations, which have shown that parts of the dike were built in earlier centuries and that Offa was not the only king to have fortified this border with Wales.

Despite its storied and no doubt bloody past, there are no surviving legends of ghosts associated with the earthwork itself. Parapsychologists claim this is because Offa's Dyke is too old. The generally held theory about ghosts by people who believe in them is that they are residual energies of living people that fades with time. This is why people claim to see ghosts of the recently departed or those who have died in the past few centuries. There are few reports of Roman ghosts, and even medieval ghosts tend to be rare and rather nebulous. If the original builders and defenders of Offa's Dike ever haunted the 1,200-year-old structure, they have likely long since faded away.

However, if the tales are to be believed, this hasn't kept spirits in the area from appearing to the living. In the woods enclosing portions of the trail, hikers have heard the clash of arms echoing through the trees, like the sounds of ancient swordfights. Some have even seen the vague forms of men in armor carrying medieval weapons. There was so much fighting on this tumultuous borderland that some ghosts seem to have lasted longer than usual.

As far as proper castles go, they have no shortage of ghosts. Raglan Castle in Monmouthshire, southeast Wales is one of the country's most spectacular castles, and like many castles in the region, it has its roots in Norman times as a motte-and-bailey castle. The Normans started building these forts right after the conquest of 1066, and most consist of an artificial hill with a wooden palisade and square wooden keep atop it. At the foot of the artificial hill was another area, enclosed by a wooden palisade, with the entire fortification surrounded by a ditch. These castles were quick and cheap to build and proved difficult for the Welsh, who lacked siege technology, to take. The Normans built them all over their newly-conquered lands, and later generations strengthened the more important ones with stone walls and towers, turning them into proper castles.

The present Raglan Castle was started in 1432 by Sir William ap Thomas, a veteran of the Battle of Agincourt, who built a fine castle of stone. It included a fortified house with two courtyards, a six-sided tower surrounded by a moat, and a stout gatehouse. His successors expanded the castle, but in 1492, the castle passed to the Somerset family. As generations of upkeep continued, one 16th century writer, Thomas Churchyard, wrote of Raglan Castle in "The Worthiness of Wales."

"The Earle of Penbroke that was created Earle by King Edward the four bult the Castell sumptuously at the first

Not farre from thence, a famous castle fine

That Raggland hight, stands moted almost round

Made of freestone, upright straight as line

Whose workmanship in beautie doth abound

The curious knots, wrought all with edged toole

The stately tower, that looks ore pond and poole

The fountaine trim, that runs both day and night

Doth yield in showe, a rare and noble sight"

Henry Somerset was the earl at the castle when the English Civil War broke out in 1642, pitting supporters of King Charles I against supporters of Parliament. The Somerset family was strongly royalist and even invited the king over to play bowls in the castle's fine gardens.

Bob McCaffrey's picture of the front façade of Raglan Castle

However, those lazy days weren't to last, as parliamentary forces soon got the upper hand. They arrived at Raglan Castle in 1646, during which the earl barricaded himself and a large force inside while parliamentarians cut the castle off from the outside world, digging siege-works. Both sides had artillery and traded fire. After two months with no relief in sight, the earl, now a marquess, surrendered, thanks to his loyalty to the king.

This started a chain of events that still echoes through the centuries. The castle had a sumptuous library filled with rare, early volumes of Welsh lore and history, and so important was this library that the castle had its own librarian tasked with studying and protecting the collection. Fearing what might happen to the precious books at the hands of parliamentarian soldiers, the librarian is said to have taken the most valuable books and hidden them away in a secret tunnel.

The librarian's caution was justified, because when the victorious troops marched in, they plundered the place, wrecking the library and destroying or stealing every book on which they could lay their hands. They also wrecked the castle walls so they could never again be used for the purpose of defense. The castle's great tower was smashed, to the extent that it now stands with half of it missing, the rooms open to the elements. A walk through the castle today brings the visitor past many gaping holes in the walls and many roofless chambers.

A picture of the state apartments (left) and library room (center)

Andy F.'s picture of the castle's tower

Some visitors to the library, now a shadow of its former self, have seen the faint image of a man dressed in 17th century clothing. He often stands in a far corner, beckoning to those who see him. Some get the sensation he wants to show them something. None have dared to follow, however, and the secret of the books' hiding place remains undiscovered to this day.

After the castle was conquered, the Marquess of Somerset was imprisoned and soon died. On his deathbed, he was told that he would be buried in the family vault back in Raglan, prompting him to quip, "Why, then, I shall have a better castle when I am dead than they took from me when alive." Presumably, he was unaware of what had happened to his castle or his beloved books.

Another haunted castle with Norman roots is Carew Castle in South Pembrokeshire. Located on strategic ground guarding the Carew River, it was an important fortification even in the prehistoric Iron Age, when there was an earthwork fortress there. Traces of a Roman settlement have been found, too, dating to before the Normans came and built a castle on the spot. After the Norman conquest, it remained an important defensive structure for another 500 years.

The first stone castle at this location was the work of Gerald of Windsor, who married Nest, Princess of Deheubarth, in 1095 and received the land as a part of her dowry. He started constructing a stone keep on the site in the year 1100. Nest was not a maiden – she had an illegitimate child with the future King Henry I - but Gerald didn't seem to mind this because the princess was rich and so beautiful that she was dubbed "Helen of Wales" after the famous Helen of Troy.

Gerald seemed to enjoy life in his new castle with his new wife, and she bore him five children in the first nine years of their marriage, but Princess Nest's beauty attracted other men. Most didn't dare defy Gerald, but one, Owain ap Cadwgan, Prince of Ceredigion and a distant relation to the princess, became so enthralled by her charms that he assembled an army and attacked the castle. After a sharp fight, Owain ap Cadwgan's men broke through the gate, and the prince rushed to the bedchamber into which Gerald and his wife had locked themselves.

Knowing it was only a matter of time before the prince and his men got inside, Nest begged her husband to escape, certain that while she was not likely to be killed, he certainly would be. The question was over how to escape, because the window led to a sheer drop, and if the fall didn't kill him, Owain ap Cadwgan's men certainly would. Instead, Nest shoved her husband down the one place the attackers were least likely to look: the privy. Toilets in castles were pretty nasty affairs, and usually, a simple wooden bench with a hole in it led from a vertical shaft to a horrific cesspool or into the moat. Gerald wormed his way down the stinky shaft to humiliating safety as Owain ap Cadwgan broke in to claim his prize.

One can only wonder exactly how unwilling Princess Nest was, since she lived with Owain ap Cadwgan for some time without a struggle and bore him two children. It was only after persistent threats from her former lover, now King Henry I, that the Prince of Ceredigion let her go. Seething with anger at being shown-up as a coward, Gerald bided his time, waiting for a chance to strike. He got it several years later, when he and his troops caught the prince in the countryside with only a light guard and cut them all to pieces.

The present castle dates to the early 14th century with additions in 15th century, during which it became more of a fortified manor house with luxurious accommodations while still serving as a fort with high walls overlooking the river.

The castle Gerald built is long gone except for the original keep, known now as the "Old Tower," but many visitors claim his beautiful wife has not departed. Princess Nest, known as the "White Lady," can still be seen floating through the hallways and along the battlements, which is unusual for a ghost. Generally, a spirit will not move into later structures, but the White Lady does not seem to mind, having visited both the Old Tower that she had once called home and the newer towers and walls built in centuries long after her death.

During the English Civil War, the owner of the castle was Sir George Carew, who, like most of the landed gentry, supported the king. His ownership was not to last, because it was soon taken by a parliamentarian force. The royalists retook it, only to lose it again. It was "slighted" at the end of the war, partially destroyed to prevent it from being used for defensive purposes.

But the strange story of Carew Castle was not yet over. One 17th century owner of the castle, Sir Roland Rhys, was a bit mad. He was a recluse, hardly seeing anyone and neglecting his manorial duties. Instead, he hid himself away in the northwest tower, his only companion a Barbary Coast ape. Thus, Sir Roland's son was left to do as he pleased, and he caused quite a lot of trouble in the neighborhood. One local girl had caught his eye, and he seduced her. The girl had caught his heart, too, and they decided to elope.

The outraged father, a Flemish merchant, went to visit Sir Roland in his eyrie and gave him a good tongue-lashing. Sir Roland was a recluse for a reason - he did not like people, and he certainly did not like being shouted at by a commoner, so he ordered his ape to attack the merchant. The beast fell upon him, fangs and claws tearing at his flesh, and the poor merchant barely escaped with his life. As he ran off, he laid a curse upon Sir Roland's head. Sir Roland didn't pay much attention to the curse, but that night, as he quietly sat in the northwest tower, the ape suddenly leaped up and attacked him. Sir Roland was made of sterner stuff than the Flemish merchant, and he struggled with the ape in an epic fight, turning over furniture and crashing against walls. By the time the servants had rushed in to see what was going on, both Sir Roland and the ape lay dead in a giant pool of blood.

Although the castle is now a partial ruin, the northwest tower still stands, and sometimes, on quiet nights, the wild howling of an ape can be heard from the top of the tower, its inhuman rage resounding across the countryside for miles around.

Today, Carew Castle is a tourist attraction still owned by the Carew family. The great empty halls and towering walls make a forbidding sight by the riverside, and bats nest in the high, echoing towers, adding a further air of gloom to the ruins. It is the perfect place to visit on a moonless night.

M. Packwood's picture of the Tudor era castle

Another picture of the current castle

Haunted Welsh Houses

Of course, historic castles are hardly the only places people think are haunted. One home that has long been considered haunted is Llanthony Secunda Manor. This large, stone building in Caldicot in Monmouthshire, southeast Wales, dates to the reign of King Henry I in the 12th century, and while it has undergone various renovations over the centuries, the foundations and walls have remained mostly the same. It was first used as a farmhouse for monks who worked land in the area. Back then, most monasteries were large farms, supporting themselves by living off the land while the monks combined daily labor with daily devotions.

This was the Augustinian monks' third attempt to build a monastery. First, they built Llanthony Priory in another location in Monmouthshire in the early years of the 12th century. The local Welsh didn't like the monks, however, and repeatedly attacked them, so in 1135, they moved to a spot just outside the English town of Gloucester and built Llanthony Secunda ("second Llanthony"). At around the same time, another priory of the same name was set up in Monmouthshire, and this is the one now believed to be haunted.

In the 16th century, the notorious King Henry VIII confiscated the building as part of his seizure of church property across his domain following his split with the Catholic Church. He does not, however, appear to have visited the place, and he soon gave it to a loyal supporter. It has remained in private hands ever since, and it is now open to guests, but a night there may not prove restful, because the monks are supposedly restless. People have reported hearing chanting in the rooms, and sometimes the shadowy image of a cowled figure is seen walking the halls. There's also a White Lady, a familiar apparition in the British Isles. This woman—either clad all in white or perhaps white due to her status as a ghost—glides through the rooms. Guests sometimes experience sensations such as the sudden feeling of being watched or followed, while others feel a light touch on their skin.

More modern homes can have paranormal activity, too. In 2014, Keiron and Tracey Fry began being terrorized in their three-bedroom, terraced house in New Tredegar in the Rhymney Valley, Caerphilly County Borough. Tracey would wake up in the morning in agonizing pain with bruises covering her back, but how they got there is a mystery since she would sleep the whole night through. While one might think the obvious answer was that Keiron was beating his wife, both of them claim this is not happening. In addition, no accusations of abuse have been made by anyone else, including the three children who live with them. It would also not explain how Keiron could have beaten his wife without waking her, or why he would seek publicity about the story by giving interviews to the press. Abusive spouses tend to be secretive and anxious to keep outsiders from prying into family affairs.

The couple claims the poltergeist began attacking Tracey about a year after they moved in on Halloween night. At first, they would hear the sound of someone or something running up and down the stairs, and glasses would fly across the room and shatter against the wall. Then Tracey started waking up injured. The attacks grew worse, and when the children heard a disembodied voice telling them, "I'm going to slit your parents' throats," it prompted the couple to bring in a paranormal expert. The expert had the family stay downstairs while he went up to the first floor where the attacks had happened. There, he encountered three demons, all of them incubi, the male form of succubus demons, who go to people at night and sexually assault them. Since Tracey had said she was only physically attacked, this entity was much more likely to be a poltergeist. A poltergeist is a particular kind of entity. Some say it is a ghost, while others claim it to be a different creature altogether. Poltergeists do not visually appear, but rather make themselves known by moving or throwing objects and making sounds, like rapping on walls and furniture. Indeed, the word itself comes from the German for "noisy spirit."

The "expert" proceeded to "kill" two of the demons, something which most demonologists say is impossible. According to them, since demons are spirits and not living things, they can only be banished. Whatever the expert did or did not do, the attacks continued just as much as before. The local vicar also came to try and get the entity to depart but met with no success. The couple had even taken a photo of one of the demons in their sons' bedroom, an image showing a small bundle of white standing at the foot of an unmade bed in a messy room. They say it is a small figure with a white hood, blue face, and tail. It could just as easily have been a bundle of clothing or sheets.

It's hard to know what to make of this story. Is this an unusual case of wife beating, where the perpetrator seeks publicity? Is it an incubus that, for some reason, only physically attacks its victims? Is it a poltergeist? Some skeptics say the whole story is false and that they are merely publicity seekers, but journalists have photographed the real bruises covering Tracey's back. It seems unlikely she would do this to herself for the dubious distinction of being the subject of a ghost story in the press.

One of the distinctions between a poltergeist and a ghost is that poltergeists tend to haunt particular individuals, rather than places. If the person moves house, the poltergeist goes with them. This has led to a discussion among parapsychologists as to whether poltergeists are spirits of the dead, as some claim, or energy given off by the individual they torment.

Whatever the explanation, Fred Matthews of Cardiff seems to be an example of poltergeists attaching themselves to individual people. Fred and his brother, John, along with John's wife, Pat, opened a mechanics shop called Mower Services on a Cardiff back street in the 1980s. The shop prospered for a while. They built up a regular customer base, enjoyed a brisk trade, and hired several employees to help with the increased workload. Then the poltergeist moved in.

It first announced its presence when the brothers were working on a car alone in the shop. Suddenly, they heard a loud racket on the metal roof. Thinking some local kids were throwing rocks on the roof to play a trick on them, Fred went out to shout at them, only to find the sound had stopped and no one was around. As soon as he went back inside, the banging on the roof started again.

It wasn't long before more strange occurrences happened. Objects such as car keys disappeared, and their owners searched all over for them until suddenly an unseen force threw the keys at them. Money disappeared from the till and was found stuffed into cracks in the wall. Strange smells would suddenly fill the room, and the temperature fluctuated wildly.

Fred and John took it all with good humor. The entity never hurt anyone, and they weren't afraid of it. They dubbed it "Pete the Poltergeist," and it became just another part of their daily lives.

When Pete began to throw things around the customers or make a visitor ask what that strange, overpowering smell was that had come out of nowhere, the brothers worried their poltergeist might hurt their business. They and their employees decided to hold a séance, locking all doors and windows and sitting around a table, holding hands. They asked Pete to announce himself. Suddenly, a stone dropped out of nowhere and landed on the table with a loud thump. After regaining their composure, they decide to continue. One of the employees said they should write down what was going on. Pete appeared to agree because a pen dropped on the table. They asked the poltergeist to drop a series of objects they named, and each object fell on the table as they named it.

Realizing they were dealing with an intelligent—if unearthly—being, they contacted parapsychologist David Fontana, who also worked as a professor of psychology at Cardiff University. It didn't take long to convince Fontana something strange was happening at Mower Services. As soon as he walked into the mechanic's shop, a large stone flew out of an empty room, nearly hitting him.

By then, the press had gotten wind of the haunting at Mower Services, and the shop began to attract a lot of public attention. The brothers' fear was finally realized, as curiosity seekers had begun to interfere with the running of their business.

Matters finally came to a head as paranormal events occurred with greater frequency. One day, Fred and John were working in the shop when Fred noticed a strange, small figure, squatting on a high shelf. It looked like a small, thin boy, with an almost blank, featureless face and grey pallor. Fred whispered to John to take a look, but the figure had vanished by the time he had turned around. Instead, John had a large brick thrown at him, missing his face by inches.

At last, the brothers had had enough, and they moved their business elsewhere, but what they didn't know was that poltergeists attach themselves to people and not places; Pete moved in with Fred and resumed his troublemaking. Fed up, Fred hired a medium who told him that whenever the poltergeist threw something, he should break the object. He followed the medium's advice, and the paranormal events stopped within a few days.

It is unclear as to why breaking objects thrown by a poltergeist should make it go away. Perhaps it's a form of symbolic rejection, or maybe the entity had to focus so much energy on the objects to throw them in the first place, that breaking them dissipated the energy. No one knows for sure, but Fred and his wife finally got some peace, and Mower Services continued to thrive in its new location.

Another Cardiff ghost lurks in the National Museum. This imposing, neoclassical building houses a fine collection of natural history, archaeological treasures, and art, where visitors can find everything from dinosaurs to contemporary paintings. After dark, however, workers can also find the ghost of the building's architect.

Arnold Dunbar Smith (1866-1933) was one of the leading architects of his day, working on many major commissions. He built the museum in 1910 and liked his work so much that he asked to be cremated and interred in the museum when he died. This was done, but some years later, the building was remodeled and Smith's ashes were moved to another location to make way for some toilets. The dead architect apparently took exception to this and began stalking the museum at night, moving objects around and shaking furniture. A paranormal investigator went in one night to try to communicate with the ghost and heard a disembodied voice muttering angrily, "The wrong place! The wrong place!"

Even quite recent buildings have been subjected to haunting. The Wales Millennium Centre in Cardiff, so named because it was supposed to have been opened in the year 2000, had a very odd and highly publicized event shortly after it opened to the public. Like many government projects, it was late in finishing and didn't have its inauguration until 2009. Even then, the inauguration festival was quickly overshadowed by a strange discovery on Google Street View - people looking up the road just outside the center spotted what looked for all the world like Mary Poppins crossing the street. Newspapers and news websites picked up the story, and it gained national attention.

Some people suspected a hoax, while others said it could be the ghost of a woman wearing clothing from a century before. They pointed out that the area was quite rough before it was revitalized, with thefts and murders being commonplace. Soon, tales began to circulate of workers hearing strange noises and seeing ghostly figures as they built the Millennium Centre, and how visitors felt a baleful presence and the sensation of being watched or followed.

Eventually, Google quashed the rumors by admitting they had dressed an actress up as Mary Poppins and had her cross the street in front of the Millennium Centre while the Google Street View car passed by. They had put several fictional characters into the app, including Paddington Bear on Portobello Road in London, and Sherlock Holmes in Oxford.

Haunted Welsh Inns and Pubs

The Welsh love a good drink, and pubs have long been popular venues where local communities can get together to relax. It seems that the spirits of the departed like hanging out in pubs just as much as the living do.

The Thomas Arms Hotel in Llanelli, Carmarthenshire is one such pub. This fine old establishment, which has been serving drinks and welcoming guests since 1830, has had the reputation of being haunted for some time now. The ghost seems to lurk in the old cellar, where the kegs and other supplies are stored. Many workers have experienced an overwhelming feeling of dread while down there, refusing to enter as they try to get other employees to fetch the kegs. Another hotspot is the stairs, where pub landlord David Langley-Evans reported to *Wales Online* in 2014 that he had the feeling of being chased.

There have also been disturbances in room six, where knocks, bumps, and other loud noises keep the guests awake all night. Sometimes, small, mysterious orbs of light float around various rooms. Orbs are a common occurrence in haunted places. Some paranormal investigators say these are the visual manifestations of spirits.

In 2014, the landlord's tales got some stunning confirmation. CCTV video of the front hallway appeared to show a nebulous, white cloud form on the floor and creep toward a sofa. The cloud began to thicken as the floor behind it became less visible, and then the cloud stretched out. There was the hint of a human shape with a body, shoulders, and head for a moment before the cloud lost shape, began to fade, and rose up to the ceiling and disappeared.

The hauntings at the Thomas Arms Hotel pale in comparison to those at the Skirrid Mountain Inn at Llanvihangel Crucorney, five miles from Abergavenny. The charming, old stone house set against the backdrop of the stunning Brecon Beacons, a chain of mountains in the south of Wales, certainly seems charming at first, and the mountains are home to one of the country's most beautiful national parks, but this spot has long been a place for magic and mystery. The word "Skirrid" comes from the Welsh "Ysgyryd," meaning "shiver." The nearby mountain is called Ysgyryd Fawr ("the Great Shiver"), and the smaller spur off of it is called Ysgyryd Fach ("the Little Shiver"). They got these names, it is said, because back when Jesus was crucified, it was a single mountain. The great mountain grew so angry during the Crucifixion that it shook with anger and split in two. This folktale is memorialized in the Skirrid Inn's sign, which shows a lightning bolt hitting the mountain.

The inn is quite old, and some architectural historians believe it may even date to the Norman period, some 900 years ago. It is said to be the oldest pub in Wales and has also performed many functions over the centuries, including once being the local court. Combining a drinking den with a court was not unknown in that era; indeed, it was a practice taken up in other places and times, most notably by the infamous Judge Roy Bean of Texas who, at the turn of the last century, used to dispense justice from his saloon.

The court was located in a room on the first floor, and those condemned to die at the Skirrid Inn were given swift justice. As soon as they were found guilty and sentenced, a rope would be thrown over the thick, oaken support beam just above the dark oak staircase, and the culprit would be strung up. The staircase didn't allow for enough of a drop, so instead of the condemned man's neck snapping, he'd slowly strangle to death, with his legs flailing as the life was choked out of him. Visitors can still see the marks the rope left on the wood.

The most notorious judge to hold court there was Judge Jeffreys, who may have been the first "hanging judge." If so, he certainly earned his title. He was loyal to the crown, and after the Monmouth Rebellion against King James II was suppressed in 1685, he established his court at the inn because it had been a meeting point for local rebels. He proceeded to try many Welshmen, find them guilty, and have his guards lead them on the short walk to the top of the stairs. Once he got through the rebels, he hanged a bunch of criminals, too. Judge Jeffreys is said to have sent 180 men to their deaths on that beam.

With such a long and bloody history, it comes as no surprise that the inn is allegedly rife with ghosts, with the most prominent being Judge Jeffreys himself. He is said to lurk on the upper floor, hoping someone will come up who deserves a good hanging. The hangman, who was quite busy in life, has also remained after death. He is not seen but felt as a baleful presence on the stairs. One of the condemned has remained, as well. John Crowther, who was strung up for sheep rustling, is sometimes seen lingering around the stairs where he choked out his last breath. Two other ghosts are known by names—Father Henry Vaughn, a local clergyman, and Fanny Price, who worked in the inn during the 18th century and is often seen in room three. There is also a mysterious White Lady who appears in various spots in and around the property.

Upstairs, people report feeling like they are being strangled or suddenly experiencing a cloying fear that has no source. The most haunted room may be room one. The small bathroom there was reportedly a prison cell associated with the court, and people have felt the air go suddenly cold in there. It is here where the spectral stranglings have occurred.

Other incidents include glasses shooting across the bar and smashing against the far wall, the scent of Fanny's lavender perfume, and the tramp of marching soldiers in the courtyard outside. The inn has been the subject of several paranormal investigations, and people who specialize in such things agree it is a hotspot for paranormal activity that has few rivals in Wales.

In the north of the country, in the village of Cym in the Vale of Clwyd, stands the Blue Lion Inn, another spot of haunted hospitality. It's a popular place, being near both the Irish Sea and the stunning mountains of Snowdonia. Like many of the haunted buildings in Wales, the Blue Lion Inn has been standing for quite some time, although its use as a pub and inn is relatively new. The structure dates to the 17th century and was first used as a home for the monks who served the nearby church. It is said that a secret tunnel connected the building to the graveyard next to the church, although why the monks would want such a passage is a mystery that is perhaps better left unsolved. They didn't need it to bury their dead, because according to local folklore, the monks were buried in tombs within the walls of their home.

The monks soon moved on, and by the middle of the 17th century, the building was used as a farmhouse. In 1646, the Henry family lived there. One of the farmer's adult sons, John Henry, suddenly disappeared. His father assumed he had left Cym because he had often expressed a desire to do so, but he felt hurt the young man hadn't thought to say goodbye. His hurt increased exponentially when his son's body was found. Some workmen in the nearby churchyard noticed the soil on a recently dug grave had been disturbed. On a grim hunch the grave had been tampered with, they dug down to find John Henry's fresh body lying on top of the coffin. He had been murdered, and the case was never solved.

As is the case with many murder victims who never got justice, John Henry's spirit was unable to leave Earth. He is sometimes seen in and around his old home as the faint image of a young man in humble, old-style clothing.

Another ghost that haunts the Blue Lion is that of the Blue Lady. Her real name and the reason for her lingering in this world are not known. She is seen in various places around the building—appearing as an elderly lady in blue—and she does not appear to be a malevolent ghost, although that doesn't stop witnesses from being terrified at the sight of her. On one occasion, a young boy was lying on his bed in one of the guest rooms when the Blue Lady suddenly appeared, lay down beside him, and told him she felt tired. Perhaps not surprisingly, he didn't stay in the room for long.

The owners and staff of the Blue Lion Inn have reported many strange occurrences. One of the strangest involved Mr. Evans, a former owner of the inn. He wasn't the most normal fellow himself, keeping a small menagerie behind the bar in several cages containing a collection of snakes, a monkey, and an alligator. They certainly made good conversation pieces for the drinkers. One morning in 1969, he arrived to get the pub portion of the inn ready for opening when he discovered all the cages open. The snakes, monkey, and alligator had spent the night wandering around the bar, causing all sorts of damage. Evans managed to get all the animals back in their cages, cleaned up the place, and opened for business.

The next night the same thing happened, and Evans figured he was the victim of a prankster. He suspected they were animal rights activists, but if they were, why hadn't the activists liberated the animals while they were at it?

That evening, he sprinkled sand all around the cages so he could see the footprints of whoever was doing it. The next morning, he once again found all the cages open and the animals wandering around the ground floor. When he examined the sand, however, he only saw the prints of the animals. No one had approached the cages—at least, no one who had left any footprints.

A more recent occurrence showed up on the inn's CCTV footage. On the night of October 30, 2017, a camera in the pub section of the building captured a lamp moving along the bar. It had been accidentally left on the night before, and when the landlord came in the next morning, it was on the floor behind the bar. Wondering what had happened, he reviewed the footage and to his shock, saw the lamp move of its own accord for a couple of feet along the bar before crashing to the floor.

Wales' Traveling Ghosts

While we tend to think of ghosts being tied to a certain building or place, repeating the same actions like some video from the other side on a perpetual loop, some spirits are known to travel the countryside, although they tend to be located in particular regions. Some stretches of road in Wales, for example, are known to be haunted by phantom hitchhikers.

The highway near Swansea is haunted by a strange variant on this disappearing spirit. It started in 2014, when a man from Pembrokeshire reported that he was driving home one afternoon after a disappointing date. As he passed along a deserted stretch of road between St. Clears and Whitland, his disappointment turned to hope when he saw a beautiful woman in a short black dress standing by the side of the road with her thumb out. After he picked her up, she immediately began to come on to him. Wasting no time, the man drove to a rest area. While this isn't the most romantic place to have a tryst, the woman appeared too impatient to wait until they got somewhere more appropriate. As they began to fool around in the car, the man started noticing a burning smell. At first, he thought it was a cigarette, but it grew in intensity and smelled more akin to burning plastic. The stench made him choke. He struggled, but the woman pushed her tongue down his throat, making him gag. Finally, he opened his eyes and saw that the woman on top of him had transformed into an old hag with decaying skin. The man screamed and pushed her off of him, screaming hysterically, and the woman vanished. Despite his terrible ordeal, the shaken eyewitness said he had driven that same stretch of road hundreds of times since the occurrence, hoping to see the woman again in order to, he claims, call the police on her.

This is not the only such incident. Several men driving alone have suffered similar indignities. Some think the creature is a succubus, a demon that sucks the life force out of men through sex, while others think it's a strange form of ghost. It just goes to show that not only is hitchhiking dangerous, but it can be dangerous to pick up a hitchhiker.

These ladies seem to be a new twist on a popular legend: the vanishing hitchhiker. Vanishing hitchhikers have been thumbing rides since the invention of the automobile and have been seen all over the world. Most recently, there has been a spate of such incidents in Japan in the wake of the terrible tsunami of 2011 that killed more than 15,000 people. The hitchhiker tends to be a woman who asks to go to an area wrecked by the tsunami, but when the taxi driver next looks in his rearview mirror, his passenger is gone. One such incident was even caught on camera - the woman can clearly be seen on the taxi's dashcam waiting at a taxi stand, but when the taxi pulls up, the door opens and closes yet nobody gets in.

People in Wales have not only encountered vanishing hitchhikers but also vanishing ships and planes. These are ghost sightings on a massive scale, often involving dozens of eyewitnesses over large areas, and some of these sightings are well-documented because people have called the police or even the Royal Air Force.

In the 1980s and 1990s, there was a wave of sightings of a ghost airplane, but air traffic controllers, the police, and the air force could find no record or trace of them. The wave of sightings appears to have started in 1987, in Abergale on the northeast coast, when numerous locals saw a large, black transport plane of the type used by the RAF in World War II. It appeared over the town and vanished before people's eyes, despite the fact it did not fly behind a cloud or some other obstruction. One moment it was there, and the next moment it was gone. Calls to the RAF proved fruitless, as there were no such known planes in the sky.

It happened again over the nearby town of Llangernyw. This time, a group of parents was picking up their children from school when a rusty, unpainted, old plane flew close overhead. As the parents rushed their children to safety, the plane took a nosedive into the nearby valley, then pulled up sharply, managed to crest a ridge, and fly out of sight. Calls to the air force and nearby airports led to no answers.

In 1994, there was another wave of ghost plane sightings in Wrexham. Most eyewitnesses said it was a World War II era transport plane that moved silently through the air, not high overhead. While this plane usually made no sound, some eyewitnesses have heard it. A family gathering crabs on the beach heard the sound of an aircraft and looked up, only to see a large transport plane driving right at them as if to crash. Scrambling for safety, they saw the pilot look right at them and pull up at the last moment before the plane winked out of existence.

Some people think this plane is the phantom image of a Washington bomber that crashed near Llanarmon-yn-Iâl in Denbighshire in 1953, which is quite close to the sightings. It was flying low on a training run when it suddenly went into a steep dive. Eyewitnesses said the pilot tried to pull out of the dive, but the engine cut off, the rear tail section fell away, the plane crashed, and all 10 crewmen died. An RAF inquiry could not determine the reason for the crash.

An earlier vehicle that crashed with tragic consequences and left an enduring image for later years was a horse-drawn coach that met a grisly end in the 1850s. This coach and four, a common mode of transport between towns before the spread of the railway, was returning to Monmouth and ran straight into the teeth of a thunderstorm. It passed through the village of Rockfield, where the roads were slick with water. The horses could barely see through the driving rain, and the crash of lightning frightened them. Despite the driver's best efforts, the horses bolted, and the coach crashed into a wall near Ancre Hill. The coach smashed, and the passengers were flung over the wall and into a nearby field. Three died, and the rest were severely injured. Motorists driving along that stretch of road in similar conditions have seen the coach and four weaving along the road, the horses clearly terrified. The coach crashes into the wall, which is still there, and the pitiful sounds of the screaming passengers are heard through the storm. As the coach disintegrates, the entire apparition disappears.

Another ghostly vehicle from a bygone age is the phantom sailing ship off Cefn Sidan. This long, beautiful beach along Carmarthen Bay in South Wales has a notorious past, as the sand reefs in the bay have snagged many a ship, and some of these wrecks have not been accidental. In the 18th century, the area was the den of a gang of wreckers, a particular type of bandit found on the coasts of Europe at the time. They waited until dark nights, especially rainy ones where the visibility was low, and strung out lanterns to guide the ships to a safe port. In reality, they were guiding them onto the rocks or sandbars, where the ship would crash. The wreckers then swarmed on board, killed any survivors, and stole the cargo.

In recent years, beachgoers have seen some shocking sights, including sightings of a phantom sailing ship. Most of the sightings follow a similar pattern, and they generally happen during the daytime. A person or group of people will be walking along the beach, enjoying the fine stretch of pale sands with the low dunes behind and forest beyond, when they hear the faint strains of music lilting over the water. As they look out, they see a large sailing ship of the kind used 300 years ago, complete with sails and portholes for cannon. The sails are tattered like it had been in a storm or battle, and the whole ship glows an ethereal green. Usually, the ship appears to be sailing right for the beach before it winks out of view. Some people have fainted at the sight of it and had to be dragged away by their friends. Dogs shy away or start howling. Even those who have managed to keep their wits feel a strong sense of dread.

One group of friends saw it while camping on the beach. It was late at night, and they had all gone inside the tent to rest up for another day of fun. At around 2:00 a.m. in the morning, they were awoken by a creaking that sounded like an old door opening. When they got out of the tent to investigate, they saw the glowing ship, far out in the bay. The whole group stared in wonder for a full two minutes before the ship disappeared. Could this old ship have been the ghost of a ship destroyed by the wreckers, its crew replaying their last moments over and over again for all time?

Wales' Violent Spirits

Most ghosts are rather passive entities. They appear in certain places at certain times, and while they frighten the wits out of whoever is unfortunate enough to meet them, they rarely approach the living or do any real harm.

Unfortunately, this is not always the case, because some spirits that are downright malevolent or attack people.

At the turn of the last century, the mining village of Tondu in Bridgend County Borough in the southern part of Wales had one such apparition. They called it the Fighting Ghost of Tondu. The Fighting Ghost lurked around the abandoned colliery of Ynysawdre, and if seen, it would rush at people. In one incident, a dozen miners were walking by the colliery when the spirit appeared as a skeletal being with glowing eyes, wearing what looked like a shroud. It shouted, "Boo!" and sailed through the air at them. Yes, there was a time when the word, "Boo!" actually scared people. Or perhaps it was the sight of the floating, skeletal ghost that proved more frightening.

Some time later, a servant girl passing by the colliery saw the ghost wandering around inside, waving its skeletal arms and groaning in agony. Then came a more violent incident. As the *Daily Mail* breathlessly reported in an article in 1904 titled, "FIGHTING GHOST MIDNIGHT STRUGGLE WITH A SPECTRE":

> "The ghost of Tondu, Glamorganshire, has reasserted itself in the most aggressive fashion.
>
> "According to a correspondent of the *South Wales Echo*, a respectable resident of the district which the uncanny apparition haunts and terrorises [sic] was proceeding at midnight along a lonely, narrow roadway adjoining the deserted buildings and coke ovens of the abandoned Ynyshawdre Colliery—an ideal spot for ghosts—when he was actually attacked by the unnatural monster.
>
> "The gentleman is muscular, but the sight which suddenly met his gaze at the far end of a tunnel-like bridge made him turn hot and cold. An exceptionally tall, cadaverous figure was standing there. A silent, motionless sentinel, it was shrouded in white, the orthodox garb of the genuine ghost.
>
> "The head, as the frightened observer now describes it, was like a deaths-head covered with wrinkled parchment. The eyes were hollow sockets, in which was a cavernous glow. Suddenly the eerie thing advanced towards the trembling man under the bridge. It approached within twenty yards, and then swiftly glided towards him with its long arms outstretched.
>
> "It clasped him as though in a vice and then began an uncanny tussle in the darkness. The man could not grip. There seemed nothing more tangible than air, but he felt himself held as though in the folds of a python, and the glowing sockets were bent full upon him. He turned to flee, but could not escape from the power that held him. With a frantic effort he clutched again at this supernatural assailant, and it was gone.
>
> "Women and children creep indoors when nightfall comes, and bands of stalwart men sally forth to lay the terror of Tondu."

The stalwart men never found the ghost. The last sighting was in September of 1904, and after that, the ghost seems to have gone back to wherever it had come from.

Another violent ghost haunted Cwmbran in 1884. He lurked in a private residence and appeared to be a gentleman wearing a "wide awake" hat (an old style hat that looks a bit like a bowler hat with a wide brim, turned up at the sides), coat, and vest, along with moleskin trousers. The woman living in the house said that it would tap the walls, whistle, and sometimes appear before her saying he'd "cut off her bloody head." A policeman was called and witnessed the ghost, which vanished before it could be arrested.

An earlier ghost spotted at Llangeler was fond of throwing stones. An old account from 1911 told the following tale:

> "In the parish of Llangeler, Carmarthenshire, May 21st., 1719, a spirit, which continued for some time, began to throw stones at those who were in the field. On Thursday in Whitsun week, at eight in the morning, the thrashing began (at a farm) and at the same time he (the spirit) began to throw stones. At first it was one of the men who were thrashing that noticed a stone descending on the thrashing floor. The second stone fell on the leg of the housemaid, wounding her; and after this, very shortly, they filled the thrashing floor and the place around. The men who were thrashing gave up their work, and went to see who were throwing them, but could see no one.

> "Friday. The servant maid in the garden was struck three times. Several of the children were struck till they went out of the house. A large number of people came together to see these wonders, and all who came were allowed to see the stones descending.

> "Saturday. The servant maid and one of the thrashers were struck. Some of the stones were rattling, and something like marks on several of them. The stones were not seen till they fell, and when they were taken up marks of them were on the floor as if they had been there from the year before. A large pole came right across the window without any one visibly bringing it. Some people believed not, till they sent messengers to see, and to bring home some of the stones to their houses. A big stump of wood was taken up from the boiler to the house top, and fell in another place.

> "Sunday. A large number of people came together to see, and several of them cursing and swearing, and speaking lightly and blasphemously. Big stones fell on the loft of the house, but were not seen till they had descended. An iron bar was struck out of the window, and another one bent as a packsaddle's hook; and the window was broken all to pieces. After dark the stones came into the beds, and window frames went to the loft, so that the family of the house were obliged to get up from their beds and go to a neighbour's [sic] house. Nothing but stones could be seen filling the house and surrounding it.

> "Wednesday Night. The barn and the corn as well as many other things were burnt; he (the spirit) was throwing stones every day, though not every hour. Sometimes the stones were thrown as fast as one could reckon them, most of

which were river stones, and some of them weighing about seven pounds or more. Neighbours [sic] came together to pray to God in the house, and there was not much noise in the house that night. Many other things were done by the spirit, but he at last ceased."

This violent spirit sounds more along the lines of a poltergeist than since it remained unseen as it threw objects. If it was a poltergeist, then it was the most active poltergeist in recorded history, since no other account ever asserted that this type of spirit filled a room with stones.

The Pit of Ghosts

During the Industrial Revolution, much of the nation's wealth came from its rich mineral deposits, especially coal. Factories all over the British Isles had an insatiable thirst for coal. London's famous fog was as much coal smoke as it was mist.

A colliery was the worst place to work during the Industrial Revolution. Miners were often killed in cave-ins, from poisonous gas emitted from the ground, and explosions. Even those who escaped these disasters could expect to suffer from black lung as the coal particulates ravaged their lungs, and quick aging as the intense physical labor racked their bodies. Moreover, it wasn't just the grown men who were working the mines, because boys as young as 9 or 10 would be given jobs below the earth, suffering even more than their fathers and uncles with their growth being stunted and their health destroyed before they had even passed through puberty. On the other hand, coal mining paid relatively well compared to factory work, and it was often the only job available in the little valley towns of Wales where the coal mines were located.

One of the most dangerous coal mines was the Morfa Colliery in Taibach near Port Talbot in southern Wales. It opened in 1844 and was producing 400 tons of coal a day at the peak of its output, but all of this came at a cost. In 1858, an explosion killed four miners. Another 30 died in a second explosion in 1863, and seven years later, another 29 died. These explosions occurred because the natural gases released by the coal could be flammable and were made worse by the coal dust in the air. Miners had no electric lights and used carefully sealed lanterns to keep them from causing explosions, but sometimes, there would be accidents, the result of someone not properly sealing his lantern or a spark from a pick hitting a stone and igniting the air. The explosions could blast out entire sections of the mines, causing cave-ins. Sometimes the coal vein would ignite, and if the fire became too extensive, the only way to douse it was to flood the mine.

On March 10, 1890, Morfa Colliery had the worst disaster in its history. A huge detonation ripped through the mine, taking the lives of 87 people. Oddly enough, the miners had been expecting it. They had reported strange noises and visions down in the depths of the mine and claimed the spirits of dead miners were trying to communicate with them to warn them of impending disaster.

All of this was reported in the newspapers of the time. The *South Wales Daily News*, in its March 12, 1890 edition, reported, "Strange as it may appear, it is beyond a doubt that the belief has for a long time been entertained by the Morfa workmen that the pit was haunted. It has been said by reliable men that there were strange noises heard 'like thunder in a distance, and the slamming of air-doors' during the last week, and strange visions alleged to have been seen in the colliery. This was the talk of the neighbourhood [sic] previous to the sad occurrence, and was the subject of conversation among the workmen before going in on Monday morning, several hours before the disaster took place. It is further alleged two or three weeks ago several workmen left the pit because of these 'visions,' which they regarded as presentiments of coming evil, and went to work in the Maesteg and other valleys."

Two days later, *The Cambrian* reported, "Morfa Colliery has been infested with restless spirits for about a week. They are supposed to be six in number, and to be the ghosts of some miners who were killed in an explosion. They make their presence known by wailing and knocking all over the underground workings. These diversions, it is said, they vary by the singing of dirges and the roll of muffled drums."

While this could be put down to journalistic creativity in order to make an already dramatic story even more dramatic, there is strong indication that it is true. The *South Wales Echo* reported on the inquiry into the disaster in its April 30, 1890 edition: "One singular incident was related in the course of the inquiry. Some short time before the explosion the men asked for a thorough inspection of the mine. Several of the witnesses were questioned as to the reasons for this request. The answer was that the men thought there were spirits in the mine. Strange sounds had been heard, and it was believed that something would be seen at the bottom of the Cribbwr vein. In short, an impression prevailed that the mine was haunted, and that an inspection would put the spirits to flight."

The *Times* on March 12 gave a more dismissive report: "The rumours [sic] which have been current that the mine is haunted probably had their origin from the fact that the workings extend to the sea and the rumbling noise is such as is frequently heard in underground workings when the sea is rough. One miner is said to have been so frightened by these noises that three weeks ago he refused to go underground and continued to the last firm in his refusal, saying that he heard similar noises when the explosion of 1870 occurred, and he had a presentiment that a like disaster could not be far off again."

It's interesting that even this skeptical interpretation admits that the men had a premonition of their own disaster. Did the spirits of the dead come to warn their living coworkers of the disaster to come? Only the poor men and boys who died that day know the truth.

Just Plain Weird

Wales may be unique in having a strange twist on the headless horseman: the two-headed ghost. This strange apparition was spotted in Abersychan in 1856, near the Blue Boar Inn. According to a local newspaper report, it was the ghost of an old man who had fallen down the stairs and split his skull. Since he had been an apostate from the Catholic Church in life, he was doomed to forever wander the Earth.

A laborer, named Dan Harley, saw it one night and was so weakened by the fear that his friends and loved ones were convinced he would die. Harley was convinced of this, too, and gave away all of his valuables. Luckily, he recovered, and his friends were kind enough to return the heirlooms to him, probably with the agreement that they would get them again when Harley really did die.

Then, there is the strange case of the headless dog that haunts the coastal village of Penparcau, just south of the city of Aberystwyth on the west coast. The dog is heard and occasionally seen on dark nights, pitifully howling as it looks for its lost master and its lost head. It is the subject of an old folktale, recorded in the 1930 volume *Welsh Folklore and Folk Custom*: "Maelor, a Cardiganshire giant, with his three sons, Cornipyn, Grugyn and Bwba, lived near Aberystwyth. One day, Maelor was caught by his enemies at Kyfeliog, some twelve miles from his stronghold. Being overcome, his request to be allowed to blow his horn thrice before being put to death was granted him. The first time he blew until his hair and his beard fell off, the second until the nails fell off his fingers and toes, and the third until the horn was shattered. Cornipyn, hearing the sound of the horn, understood what was happening, and sorrow for his father came upon him at a place still known as Cefn Hiraethog (hiraeth, longing). As he rode to the rescue, his dog failed to keep pace with him, and its head came off in the leash at Bwlch Safn y Ci, 'the Pas of the Hound's Mouth.' Cornipyn made his horse leap the valley, landing at a spot named Ol Carn y March, 'the Steed's Hoofmark.' Coming to his father, he was also killed. The two other brothers were afterwards killed through cunning." While one might think this is only quaint folklore from a bygone age, the dog is still encountered to this day, with sightings as recent as 2016.

Other strange creatures have been spotted in this region, and the village of Penparcau was part of a larger mystery in 1855. The winter of that year was a severe one, and on the night of the February 8, it snowed heavily across the south of England and Wales. The next morning in Devon, southwest England, the villagers and farmers saw some strange prints in the snow. One news report that was sent around the world tells of what they saw: "It appears on Thursday night last, there was a very heavy snowfall in the neighbourhood [sic] of Exeter and the South of Devon. On the following morning the inhabitants of the above towns were surprised at discovering the footmarks of some strange and mysterious animal endowed with the power of ubiquity, as the footprints were to be seen in all kinds of unaccountable places—on the tops of houses and narrow walls, in gardens and court-yards, enclosed by high walls and pailings, as well in open fields."

The tracks looked like horseshoes but were smaller than a horse or a pony. The prints ran along fields, along the tops of houses and walls, and through enclosed gardens. The creature or spirit or whatever it was could leap onto tall buildings and pass wide rivers. The tracks were followed for more than 100 miles into Devon. The tracks became instantly famous as "the Devil's footprints," and caused much speculation by naturalists and put much fear in the hearts of Devonshire parishioners. What is less known is that they were also found in Penparcau, more than 100 north and across the Bristol Channel. Like the prints in Devon, these were of a small, hoofed entity, able to pass over houses and high walls with ease. It appears the devil, or spirit, had walked longer than the good folks of Devon had realized.

Then there was an unusual mermaid sighting, if indeed it was a mermaid. It was mentioned in the Welsh newspaper, *Seren Gomer,* in 1833:

> "In the month of July, 1826, a farmer from the parish of Llanllwchaiarn, about three miles from Aberystwyth, whose house is within 300 feet of the seashore, descended, the rock, when the sun was shining beautifully upon the sea, and he saw a woman (as he thought) washing herself in the sea within a stone's throw of him. At first, he modestly turned back, but after a moment's reflection thought that a woman would not go so far out into the sea, as it was flooded at the time, and he was certain that the water was six feet deep in the spot where he saw her standing. After considering the matter, he threw himself down on his face and crept on to the edge of the precipice from which place he had a good view of her for more than half-an-hour.

> "After scrutinizing her himself, he crept back to call his family to see this wonderful sight. After telling them what he had seen, he directed them from the door where to go and to creep near the rock as he had done. Some of them went when they were only half dressed, for it was early in the morning, and they had only just got up from bed. Arriving at the spot, they looked at her for about ten minutes, as the farmer was calling his wife and the younger child. When the wife came on, she did not throw herself down as the others had done, but walked on within sight of the creature; but as soon as the mermaid saw her, she dived into the water, and swam away till she was about the same distance from them as she was when she was first seen.

> "The whole family, husband, wife, children, menservants and maid-servants, altogether twelve in number, ran along the shore for more than half-a-mile, and during most of that time, they saw her in the sea, and sometimes her head and shoulders were upwards out of the water. There was a large stone, more than a yard in height, in the sea, on which she stood when she was first seen. She was standing out of the water from her waist up, and the whole family declared that she was exactly the same as a young woman of about 18 years of age, both in

shape and stature. Her hair was short, and of a dark colour; her face rather handsome, her neck and arms were like those of any ordinary woman, her breast blameless and her skin whiter than that of any person they had ever seen before.

"Her face was towards the shore. She bent herself down frequently, as if taking up water, and then holding her hand before her face for about half-a-minute. When she was thus bending herself, there was to be seen some black thing as if there was a tail turning up behind her. She often made some noise like sneezing, which caused the rock to echo. The farmer who had first seen her, and had had the opportunity of looking at her for some time, said that he had never seen but very few women so handsome in appearance as this mermaid. All the family, the youngest of whom is now eleven years old, are now alive, and we obtained this account, word for word, as it is given here, from them themselves within the last month."

While this report fits more into the field of cryptozoology, that of studying as of yet unidentified species, some ghost hunters have pointed to the account of the mermaid's white skin, an unusual feature in descriptions of mermaids, and say that the family was most likely seeing the ghost of a mermaid. Other animals have returned from the dead as ghosts, so why not a mermaid?

It's certainly no stranger than the phantom cow that supposedly haunts a field off the old Abergavenny Road in Monmouthshire. Several milkmaids working that farm have reported seeing it when going out in the early morning to milk the herd. At such an early hour, many of the cows are still asleep. Contrary to popular belief, cows do not sleep standing up, and thus cannot be tipped. They sleep lying down, and the best way to wake them is to give them a hard slap on the rump. This works on children and lazy spouses, too.

Every now and then, however, the milkmaid would slap a cow, and her hand would pass right through it before the cow vanished. The nearby farmhouse is haunted, as well, with strange noises as of people moving and lights that go on and off without anyone touching the switch.

On September 2, 1905, in Froncysyllte in north Wales, numerous witnesses spotted what appeared to be a large pig with wings flying high overhead. The animal was 10 feet long, about two miles up, and clearly visible only through powerful binoculars. The *Cambrian Natural Observer*, the journal of the Astronomical Society of Wales, reported, "We are told that it had short wings, and flew, or moved, in a way described as 'casually inclining sideways.' It seemed to have four legs, and looked to be about ten feet long. According to several witnesses it looked like a huge, winged pig, with webbed feet."

As the old adage puts it, people always say they'll believe something when pigs fly, and some Welshmen actually claim they have.

Haunted Castles

Scotland's past was a violent one, from bitter struggles between Highland clans to invasions from England and Scandinavia, resulting in a landscape filled with castles. From small family forts to massive military establishments and royal domains, Scotland is estimated to have some 3,000 castles. Many of these have witnessed violent sieges, political prisoners walled up in dungeons and allowed to starve to death, and bloody family feuds. Is it any wonder that so many of Scotland's castles have a reputation for being haunted?

One castle with a long history of hauntings is Bedlay Castle, a few miles outside of Glasgow. Built in the late 16th century as a tower house - a fortified stone tower with living facilities - a succession of owners have expanded it over the years to make it larger and more comfortable for those who had to live there. Larger it certainly became, but not more comfortable, as generation after generation of residents have been terrorized by ghosts, such as that of a large bearded man said to be Bishop John Cameron (in office 1426-1446), one of the Bishops of Glasgow. His life ended well before the tower house was built, but there had been a residence for bishops on the site that has long since disappeared. Bishop Cameron has lingered, however, probably because his soul can't find rest. The bishop was found face down in a nearby loch, and many at the time believed he was murdered. If this is true, the killers got away, but legend has it he has wandered the area for centuries and is often seen walking into rooms in the house, perhaps in search of those who cut his life short. He is one of Scotland's most enduring ghosts.

There is also a phantom coach that travels down a nearby road between Glasgow and Sterling. It was an old coaching road in the days when horse-drawn coaches were the only form of public transport. Phantom coaches such as this are a mainstay of ghost sightings across the British Isles. In this case, the coach stops in front of the startled eyewitness, and a young girl in historic costume steps out. As soon as her foot touches the ground, the air splits with a loud scream, and the girl and the coach both disappear.

Not all the manifestations are visible. Residents in the castle have complained of hearing footsteps down empty corridors and feeling invisible fingers touch their hair.

In his 1856 book *Rambles Around Glasgow*, folklorist Hugh MacDonald discusses the ghost of the bearded man in skeptical detail:

> "Bedlay House has, or at least had, the unenviable reputation of being haunted. Who or what the ghost was while in the flesh we have been unable to discover, but that something uncannie [sic] had been seen or heard about the place is, or we should perhaps say was, very generally believed over the neighbourhood [sic]. One old man informed us seriously that it was a bad laird of former days who could not get rest in his grave. 'He was a sair trouble to a' about him (quoth our informant) when he was leevin', and I think it's rather too bad that he should get leave to come

back and disturb decent folk after he's dead.'

"According to fireside gossip[,] a party of ministers were on one occasion called in to lay the unquiet spirit; and we are assured, on the authority of an old man whose father held the reverend gentlemen's horses while they were engaged in the work, that when they came out of the house afterwards, 'the very sweat was pouring down their faces.' Whether the holy men succeeded in giving the ghost its quietus, or whether the general spread of knowledge, as is perhaps more likely, has put it to flight, we do not know, but one thing is certain, and that is, that there is now considerable doubts among the people of Chryston with regard to its existence. One gudewife, whom we question on the subject while she is filling her pitcher at Bedlay well, says, 'It's my honest opinion there was mair clash than onything else in the ghost story; and for my part I dinna believe ae word o't.'"

Later residents in the castle beg to differ because the hauntings continued throughout the 20th century.

Another haunted castle is one of Scotland's oldest. Duntrune Castle by Loch Crinan in Argyll was built in the 12th century and has the distinction of being the oldest continually inhabited castle in mainland Scotland. Standing atop a small peak overlooking the loch, it makes for an impressive sight, and for a long time, it served as one of a chain of castles built by the MacDougall clan to protect their territory, but it was later taken by the powerful Clan Campbell. This clan was constantly trying to expand its lands and made many enemies, including the Clan MacDonald. In 1644, the MacDonalds besieged the castle, and it was around this time that the castle apparently acquired its ghost.

Patrick Mackie's picture of the ruins of the castle

Macdonnel Coll Ciotach of Ulster marched with a large host through Campbell lands destroying everything in his path. Hearing that the Campbells had a stout fortress at Loch Crinan, he sent his piper to scout the castle, look for weaknesses, and report back to him. The piper pretended to be a wandering musician and asked for entry to the castle. The Campbells became instantly suspicious of his motives for visiting during wartime but admitted him—leading him straight to a cell in one of the towers. Oddly, they let him keep his pipes.

The piper had seen enough of the castle to know that his master would have no chance of taking it, so he peered out the window day and night, waiting to see Macdonnel Coll Ciotach's ships come up the loch as they had planned.

At last, the ships appeared, and the piper began to play the pibroch "The Piper's Warning to his Master." When Macdonnel Coll Ciotach heard the tune, he knew the piper was telling him to retreat, and he turned his ships around.

Of course, the Campbells had heard the pipe music, too. Realizing what the piper had done, they cut off all of his fingers so he could never play again. The piper bled to death, but ever since, the faint notes of "The Piper's Warning to his Master" can occasionally be heard through the stone corridors of the castle, sending chills up the spine of anyone who hears them.

Much later, the story had a startling confirmation when workers renovating the old castle came across a grave containing a skeleton missing both its hands, which had been cleanly cut off at the wrists, and buried according to Episcopalian rites. Many clans at the time, the MacDonalds included, were Episcopalian, but the Campbells were Presbyterian. The handless body was reinterred, but this did not stop the hauntings, and the piper continues to play his ghostly tune. In 1792, the castle and its ghostly piper were sold to Clan Malcolm, and it continues to serve as the clan seat to this day.

What hasn't changed much is the old clan territory around Loch Fyne, Argyll, on Scotland's west coast, which remains an area of natural beauty, with lonely shorelines, large areas left for animal grazing, and several little villages dotting the landscape. This has been traditional MacLachlan land for centuries, the clan stubbornly defending it against rival clans and the English. The MacLachlans also took part in many uprisings against the English as loyal Jacobites.

In 1745, rumors spread that Charles Edward Stuart had returned from exile to raise an army to fight for the Jacobite cause, which was nothing short of putting the House of Stuart back on the British throne. Everyone in Scotland—from the most powerful clan chiefs to the humblest shepherd—had to think long and hard about which side to take. The English had a much more powerful army than the clans, but for some, loyalty to the Jacobite cause was even more powerful.

Bonnie Prince Charlie

Lachlan MacLachlan, 17th chief of the Clan MacLachlan, sought the advice of Master Harry, the brownie that lived in the cellars of the castle. He was a tricky spirit, always playing pranks and scaring people, but he was also a staunch supporter of Clan MacLachlan, and in this grave hour, the clan chief knew he could trust the brownie's opinion. He found Master Harry beside himself with worry, saying that a stranger was coming from the north who would lead Lachlan to his death.

The clan chief knew the stranger must be the Bonnie Prince Charlie, Charles Edward Stuart.

Though he was worried about the brownie's words, Lachlan could not abandon the man whom he saw as the rightful king. He rallied his men and got ready to join him, but when he mounted his horse, the animal grew skittish and turned three times counterclockwise, a bad omen.

The brownie and the horse had seen the future. At the Battle of Culloden on April 16, 1746, Lachlan MacLachlan was killed by an English cannonball. Many other men of the clan fell as well. There is a mass grave on the battlefield of Culloden, with a headstone bearing the MacLachlan name. Clan lore says that Lachlan's horse galloped back to Castle Lachlan on the shore of Loch Fyne. When the residents saw the riderless horse, they knew their clan chief was dead.

Built in the 15th century, Castle Lachlan is of unusual design, with a rectangular layout, two residences, and a central courtyard within. After the English had won the battle, they set about destroying the strongholds of any clan opposing them, and old Castle Lachlan was no exception. The English sent a warship up Loch Fyne and bombarded the castle until it was a ruin. It was never rebuilt but remains an atmospheric ruin at the edge of the loch. Everyone left. Some of them were hunted by the authorities while others managed to escape. The only resident remaining at the castle was the Lachlan MacLachlan's loyal steed, which refused to leave until the day it died.

Some of the ruins of Castle Lachlan

According to lore, the horse is still there. Sometimes at night, the ruined walls of the castle echo with the sound of its whinnying and its hooves striking stone. Some hikers have even glimpsed it galloping to the castle, its saddle still empty.

Indeed, it doesn't take long to find allegedly haunted castles in Scotland, as the hauntings start just as visitors get to the border between England and Scotland. Berwick-upon-Tweed is located just over two miles south of the current border in the English county of Northumberland, and it has been fought over by the English and Scots for centuries. For much of its history, Berwick-upon-Tween was a Scottish town, and many believe it is still home to a very Scottish ghost.

Berwick Castle, which dates back to Norman times and was the scene of much of the fighting, now stands in ruins, but at least one old occupant allegedly still resides there. On moonlit nights, some people have seen a Highland bagpiper in full regalia, standing atop the crumbled battlements, playing a ghostly tune. He is most often seen standing close to a steep flight of stone steps, locally referred to as "the breakneck stairs." Is the piper commemorating the accidental death of some long-departed Scot--perhaps himself?

An 18th century depiction of Berwick Castle

The ruins of the castle today

Haunted Roads

The piper isn't the only ghost in Berwick-upon-Tweed. All three bridges spanning the River Tweed have their own ghosts. The oldest bridge, named Berwick Bridge, or by the local and not particularly original name of Old Bridge, was built in the early 17th century. At times the gray, blurry figure of a hooded monk can be seen walking across this historic span.

The Royal Border Bridge is a railway bridge built by famous railway engineer Robert Stephenson in 1850 at the dawn of the railway era. He was the son of George Stephenson, who built the world's first inter-city railway line between Liverpool and Manchester, in 1830. Robert Stephenson followed in the footsteps of his father and helped the railroad crisscross England. The Royal Border Bridge is one of his masterpieces, being 2,162 ft (659 m) long, with 28 arches rising 121 ft (37 m) above the river. Robert died in 1859, and has often been seen since, stalking the railway bridge at night, still admiring his creation.

Robert Stephenson

A third bridge, opened in 1928, is haunted by the ghost of a worker who died during its construction. It is one of the many constructions worldwide that are home to spirits of the men who died while building them.

In Scotland proper, the ghosts seemingly only get thicker. On the border, they tend to stick to travel routes and old buildings, and there are even entire stretches of roads that are considered haunted. The most notorious is the A75, especially the Kinmount Straight section in southwest Scotland, locally known as the "Ghost Road." This stretch of highway has seen numerous paranormal encounters for more than half a century.

The earliest sighting dates to 1957, when a truck driver passing along the A75 at night saw a couple walking, arm in arm, right across the road in front of him. He slammed on his brakes and was convinced he'd hit them. Once he'd pulled over, he jumped out of his vehicle to search for the bodies, but the couple had vanished.

A more dramatic apparition happened in 1962, when Derek and Norman Ferguson were driving along the road at around midnight. Suddenly, a large hen flapped up towards their windshield. The two men were startled, but not spooked. Anyone who has spent time driving in rural areas has had at least one near miss, thanks to a stray farm animal. Chasing after the hen came an old woman, waving her arms at the car. At first, the two men thought this was the owner of the animal, but then their experience got weirder. Right behind the old woman came a screaming man with long hair, followed closely by a menagerie of wild dogs, giant cats, hens, goats, and some creatures the Fergusons couldn't identify.

They didn't have long to look, as all of the people and the creatures disappeared in an instant. By this time, they had stopped the car. Suddenly, they felt the temperature plunge, and the car began to rock violently from side to side as if by an unseen force. Derek, either bravely or foolishly, got out of the car and the movement stopped as abruptly as it had started. He got back in, shaken and bewildered, only to see a large van come barreling down the street at them. It vanished just before hitting them.

The detail about the temperature going down is an interesting one. Paranormal investigators believe that ghosts draw ambient energy from the air around them, which causes the temperature to plunge. The more energy they require, the more the temperature will go down. The Fergusons felt the temperature go down quickly, just before the unseen spirits rocked their car. Some specialists in the spirits of the dead theorize that a ghost's need for energy is one of the reasons they are so rarely seen during the daytime. The power of the sun overwhelms them, it being too powerful for them to manifest in their weakened state, and thus blanks them out.

It's interesting that the ghosts that came at the Fergusons seemed to be trying to communicate with the land of the living. Garson and Monica Miller were driving at around 60 mph along the road one night in March of 1995, when suddenly a man stepped out, right in front of them. He looked to be middle aged, but rather strange. He had an empty sack folded on top of his head, and held what appeared to be a rag in his hands as he outstretched his arms towards the car. They didn't get much of a look, because they were going too fast. Like other drivers on this stretch of road, they were convinced they had hit what they'd thought was a regular human being, but when they screeched to a halt and went back to look, there was, of course, no trace of him. The couple was so concerned, they filed a police report.

The police received another baffling report in July of 1997, when Donna Maxwell was driving along the A75 with her two children. As with the other apparitions, a man stepped out into the road, right in front of her. Maxwell described him as being in his 30s with short hair, a red top, and dark pants. He, too, disappeared upon impact. She filed a police report, and apparently was so convincing, that the police didn't dismiss her story, but rather, issued a description of the man, asking the public for any clues. No one had seen the incident or reported a man with that description who had been injured in a car accident.

In another encounter back in 2012, a long-distance truck driver had parked on the Kinmount Straight portion of the A75, and took a nap in the back of his truck. The fellow must not have been a local, because no one familiar with the area would have ever considered doing that! He woke up at three in the morning with a dreadful sense of foreboding. When he looked out the window, he saw a long column of bedraggled people in what appeared to be medieval peasants' rags. Some were pushing handcarts as they trudged down the road like refugees. Others have seen this grim cavalcade, too.

The medieval refugees seem to be the only repeat performers on the A75. While hauntings in most places are typified by the same ghost appearing again and again, like the ghostly piper of Berwick Castle, the A75 ghosts are unusual for their variety, including everything from hens to eyeless phantoms.

The hauntings on the A75 Kinmount Straight fall into a pattern seen on many haunted roadways in the British Isles. Phantom travelers who suddenly disappear have been a part of road lore, probably as long as there have been roads, but with the invention of the automobile, they took on a different flavor. Now, instead of a farmer meeting a ghostly apparition at night while walking home from the May Fair or harvesting, a motorist will catch a glimpse of a ghost and think they have run it over. When they go to investigate, the ghost has disappeared. The A75 Kinmount Straight is not the only haunted road in Scotland, but it is the quintessential one.

Edinburgh

If the A75 is the most haunted road in Scotland, Edinburgh must be the most haunted city. This ancient center of Scottish life has been witness to some of the great events of Scottish history, and at the same time, has been a place of misery for many common people. Much of the central part of the city is a UNESCO World Heritage Site. Dominating the skyline is the great rocky hill atop which looms Edinburgh Castle, recently voted the top UK Heritage Attraction in the British Travel Awards. First built in the 12th century, it has been added to over the generations and is now an impressive site to visit for its fine views of the city, its several museums, and its storied past.

The city's most conspicuous landmark is Edinburgh Castle, sitting high atop a rocky eminence that dominates the surrounding countryside. It is a truly magnificent sight, having served as a defensive position since Celtic times, from at least the 2nd century AD. It started off being a fortress for the kings of Scotland, as early as the reign of King David I (1124-1153). Like many Scottish castles, it was the scene of bitter fighting on numerous occasions, having been besieged at least 26 times in its history, and perhaps more, since its early history is poorly known. Now it hosts numerous public events, and is a fascinating historic site where visitors get to see various museum displays, the Crown Jewels of Scotland, and the enormous medieval cannon, Mons Meg.

Kim Traynor's picture of Edinburgh Castle

Much of the paranormal activity in the castle comes in the form of strange sounds. Phantom drummers can be heard at night, calling the men to defend the battlements, and the castle wardens report strange knockings in locked and supposedly empty buildings. There is also a spectral piper who is heard but not seen, and a drummer who almost nobody wants to see because he's missing his head! The spirits manifest in other ways, too, such as sudden drops in temperature. Some people have also said they've felt an invisible hand tugging on their clothing, or touching their face.

At the foot of the castle is the Old Town, dating back to the early Middle Ages. Now clean and visitor-friendly, it was once a hellhole of overcrowded tenements, filthy streets, narrow lanes clogged with trash, and the occasional dead body. Space was at a premium, so most roads were narrow, and the buildings were some of the tallest of their age, rising six or more stories, leaving the narrow paths in almost perpetual darkness. Beneath this tangle of buildings is a warren of tunnels that attracted the poorest of the poor who went there in search of shelter, often dying unnoticed in the dark.

Beyond the Old Town is the newer and more orderly New Town, started in the 18th century to relieve overcrowding. An early example of urban planning, its Georgian and neoclassical architecture make for a pleasant contrast with the Old Town's more somber buildings.

Edinburgh has been home to many famous people who have left their mark on the fields of science and the arts, Alexander Graham Bell, pioneer of the telephone, was born there, as was John Napier, the mathematician who invented logarithms. Sir Arthur Conan Doyle, the creator of Sherlock Holmes, was born in New Town, and *Treasure Island* author Robert Lewis Stevenson lived there, as well. The city was also home to a fair number of murderers, thieves, and conmen, attracted by the excitement of living in a big city and its easy access to wealthy victims.

One of its more sinister residents was Major Thomas Weir. At first glance, he seemed the very model of an upstanding citizen. Born in 1599, he had a long military career before settling down in Edinburgh in his later years and becoming captain of the Town Guard. He was known throughout the town as a strict Presbyterian who never missed a church meeting, kept a chaste life, and lived with his sister, Jean (often referred to in sources as "Grizel").

They made their home on the West Bow, a curving street leading from the Royal Mile's wealthy homes and shops down to the lower town filled with slums and cheap drinking dens. Bow Street was a bastion against the low-lives from the lower town, held as such by well-to-do Presbyterians such as Major Weir, dubbed the "Bowhead Saints."

A depiction of Major Weir's house

Major Weir was a familiar sight about town with his military bearing, stern visage, and the black, Thornwood staff—carved with satyrs' heads—he always carried. These lusty pagan creatures from classical mythology were an odd choice for such a man to have on his staff, but no one thought much of it or the fact that he never failed to carry it.

One Sunday in 1670, Weir stood up to address the congregation, clutching his trusty staff as he always did, but instead of giving the usual sermon on sin and God's wrath, he shocked his fellow churchgoers with a lengthy, lurid confession of how he was a warlock. He recounted, in vivid detail, how he had been having an incestuous relationship with his sister for years. In addition, he had enjoyed carnal relations with various women and even some animals. The assembly sat and stared for a while, not believing their ears. Finally, they rose up and grabbed him. They would never have believed they had a warlock in their midst unless Major Weir had himself admitted to being one.

    The law was initially reluctant to charge a pillar of the community with such foul crimes and suggested the man had either gone insane or was senile. He was 70 years old, after all, quite an advanced age for the time, but when they questioned his sister, Jean, she backed up the tales, embellishing them with her own details of having met with the Devil and riding around the countryside in a fiery coach. She also claimed that Major Weir's black Thornwood staff with the satyrs' heads had been a present from the Devil himself and was the key to his power.

    In the face of such confessions, the court had no choice but to convict. The siblings were sentenced to execution by strangulation, which meant they were to be strapped to chairs atop a platform in front of a cheering crowd, with ropes looped through holes in the backs of the chairs that were tightened with a handle, slowly crushing the necks of the condemned. It was traditional for the executioner to tell the people to repeat the line, "Lord be merciful to me," so it would be their last statement before having the life choked out of them. Instead, Major Weir stated, "Let me alone. I will not. I have lived as a beast, and I must die as a beast." The execution proceeded, and afterward, his body was thrown into a fire to purify it. The executioner threw Weir's famous staff in after him, and many witnesses swore they saw it writhe like a snake and refuse to catch fire for many long minutes before it finally expired.

    Jean went out in a similarly dramatic fashion. As they brought her up to the scaffold and the strangulation chair, she tore off her clothes and exposed herself to the assembled onlookers.

    After their deaths, no one wanted to live in the Weirs' nice home on West Bow. It had been cursed, people whispered, and the spirits of the evil siblings still lingered there. For a hundred years before its final demolition, the property remained vacant, though the district was popular, save the activity there on some nights when lights are seen in the windows and baleful laughter resonates from within. Some have even heard the whirl of Jean's spinning wheel. What she could be spinning after death is anyone's guess. Sometimes, Major Weir makes an appearance on the street, galloping away on a headless black horse, no doubt on a mission to take care of the Devil's foul business.

    The famous author, Robert Louis Stevenson, who was born and raised in Edinburgh, remembered growing up hearing tales of the strange transformation of these two pillars of Christian society. Literary critics believe this story to be the inspiration for his famous novel, *Dr. Jekyll and Mr. Hyde*.

    Some sources say that Major Weir and his sister were the last people to be executed for witchcraft in Scotland, but this is incorrect. That dubious distinction goes to Janet Horne, who was burned at the stake for being a witch in 1727. She was also accused of riding her daughter to visit the Devil and having the girl shod like a horse. The older woman showed signs of senility, and the daughter had deformed hands and feet, sparking the imagination of superstitious neighbors who spread all sorts of accusations about the pair, claiming all of their troubles were the result of their practicing witchcraft.

Janet was stripped naked, smeared with hot tar, and paraded through the town of Dornoch in a barrel. Then she was taken to the spot where she was to be burned at the stake. The woman is said to have smiled at the crowd as she warmed herself by the fire that would soon kill her. Her daughter was also found guilty but managed to escape.

Scotland got rid of the death penalty for witchcraft nine years later, but there have been several extrajudicial killings since that time. If one walks downhill on West Bow and takes a left on Grassmarket, he or she will come to Greyfriars Kirkyard, the site of one of Scotland's most notorious poltergeists. A poltergeist is a particular kind of entity. Some say it's a ghost, while others claim it to be a different creature altogether. Poltergeists do not visually appear, but rather, make themselves known by moving or throwing objects and making sounds, like rapping on walls and furniture. The word comes from the German for "noisy spirit."

One spirit in the graveyard is noisier than any other poltergeist ever recorded. It is the shade of Sir George Mackenzie, often referred to as "Bloody Mackenzie." Born in Dundee sometime in the 1630s, Mackenzie rose to prominence in the legal profession and served as Justice-Depute between 1661 and 1663. During this time, he presided over several witch trials, and what is perhaps unusual for this era, he dismissed the charges, claiming the witches had suffered from mental illness, senility, or that they had been the victims of scurrilous rumors started by their neighbors. Modern historians agree, but it was a daring stance to take at the time. He also became a member of the Scottish Parliament for the County of Ross. In 1677, he was appointed Lord Advocate of Scotland, the highest legal position in the land, at which point, his reputation for tolerance and open-mindedness seems to have fled him.

Mackenzie

At that time, Scotland was being ripped apart by a religious struggle. A traditionalist Presbyterian movement, called the Covenanters, resisted English attempts at installing a new liturgy and eventually, Episcopalianism in Scotland. The fight had been going on for several decades, and it was Mackenzie's job to put a stop to it, solidifying England's rule over Scotland. One of the key tenets in Episcopalianism is that the monarch is the head of the Church, something to which most Presbyterians object since it smacks of Catholicism.

In 1679, matters came to a head when the Covenanters rose up in rebellion. The uprising was quickly quashed when the Covenanter Army met with defeat at the Battle of Bothwell Bridge on June 22 of that year. Hundreds of rebel prisoners were marched to Edinburgh and given over to Mackenzie and installed in Greyfriars Kirkyard, an ironic move since that's where the movement had begun at a meeting in 1638. There, the rebels stayed in what amounted to little more than an animal pen, underfed and exposed to the elements. Hundreds died of exposure and disease during the winter, with only a few surviving. The leaders were beheaded, which was at least a quick death. Their heads adorned various public squares and main roads as a grisly reminder of what happened to those who had defied the king.

Mackenzie hunted down Covenanters wherever he could find them. Some historians estimate he killed 18,000 of them in what has become known as "the Killing Time." Others say this number is highly inflated, but he certainly earned the nickname of "Bloody Mackenzie."

When it came Mackenzie's turn to die in 1691, he was installed in a fine family mausoleum only a few yards from the former site of the prison, a distinctive, circular structure of grey stone, topped with a dome. The entrance room is empty, and a narrow flight of spiral stairs winds down to where the coffins of Mackenzie and three of his relatives lie.

It was after Bloody Mackenzie was laid to rest that the hauntings began there. At first, all was quiet at the mausoleum, but it is said that a highwayman named John Hayes fled there sometime in the 18th century. On the run from the law, he hid in a place he figured no one would look for him: inside Mackenzie's mausoleum. He is reputed to have lived there for six months, only coming out to steal the occasional food and drink. Eventually, someone spotted him returning "home" from one of his foraging expeditions and informed the authorities. When they stormed in to arrest him, they found Hayes had gone completely mad, raving that the coffins would move about at night and that Mackenzie could be heard scraping at the inside of the coffin as if trying to get out.

The mausoleum was resealed and remained quiet for a time. Then, in 1998, the mausoleum was broken into again, this time by a homeless man who had wanted to get out of the rain. He passed through the first room, opened a grate to the stairs leading to the lower room where the coffins of Mackenzie and his kinfolk were kept, and went down there. As he stepped onto the lower floor, the old wood gave way, and he crashed through and into a hitherto unknown third room, landing in a viscous, rotting mass of corpses in a plague pit from one of the many epidemics that had swept through Scotland. The people had been thrown into the pit together, probably in several cartloads of corpses gathered throughout the city, before the room was quickly sealed up, which probably accounts for the preservation of the corpses. Shrieking in terror and covered in rotting flesh, the homeless man scrambled out of the pit, having decided that a night in the rain didn't sound so bad after all. He shot up the stairs and straight across the churchyard, passing by a night watchman who had come to investigate the sounds. The sight of a screaming man covered in rotting flesh made the watchman scream as well, and he ran off into the night as fast as the homeless man.

Ever since the Mackenzie mausoleum and the plague vault were disturbed on that stormy night, people have reported strange phenomena around the place. Accounts started as soon as the next day, when a local woman walking past the mausoleum noticed it had been broken into and she peeked inside, only to be blown off her feet by a cold wind. Other passersby have seen strange shadows flitting in and out of the mausoleum. Loud noises emanate from it at night, such as the sound of a heavy, wooden object being dragged over stone.

When a woman was found unconscious nearby, her neck covered in bruises she later swore had been made by an invisible assailant that tried to strangle her, the city council put a new lock and gate on the structure and posted a no trespassing sign, but it did not stop the activity around the haunted vault. Police are regularly called in to deal with people claiming to have been slapped or pinched by unseen hands. Small animals are often found sacrificed at the entrance.

Even though the vault is off-limits to the general public unless they are with an accredited guide, it stands in the middle of a public cemetery, so countless people still witness strange goings-on. Many experience cold breezes coming from out of nowhere, or spots that are inexplicably much colder than the surrounding area. The attacks from the invisible entity often leave bruises and broken fingers behind. As recently as October 20, 2017, the *Edinburgh Evening News* reported that a man there had been scratched by an invisible attacker.

The poltergeist phenomena show no signs of abating. Ghost hunters theorize Bloody Mackenzie is not the only problem, instead blaming the more recently released ghosts from the plague pit. Indeed, the hauntings seem to have become much worse since the pit's discovery than at any previous time in the mausoleum's long history. The spirits were probably stirred up even more when two teenagers, no doubt encouraged by the place's reputation, broke into the mausoleum and stole a skull. Police found them playing football with it.

What's unusual about the Mackenzie Poltergeist is that it has endured for so long and is not attached to any one particular living person. Normally, poltergeists are associated with girls going through puberty, prompting some parapsychologists to theorize they are some sort of hormonal psychic projection. The girls seem to act as focal points, and unlike what might happen in a haunted house or castle, if the girls move to another location, the hauntings move with them. All that is well and good, but pubescent boys have just as many hormones raging through their systems as pubescent girls yet are rarely associated with poltergeist phenomena. The Mackenzie Poltergeist is a rare exception in that it is focused around a particular spot and not an individual, so while the entity manifests like a poltergeist, it has many aspects of a traditional ghost.

The hauntings in Greyfriars Kirkyard are not confined to Bloody Mackenzie's mausoleum. Indeed, they can be found all across the extensive burial ground.

Walking through the burial ground is a creepy experience. The monuments date from as early as 1561, when the cemetery was founded, to the middle of the 20th century, and they serve as an outdoor museum of strange funerary art in which grey stone skulls leer at visitors, angels weep over the dead, and the likenesses of the dead peer out, their faces frozen in time. One odd feature is the mortsafe, a thick iron cage built around the burial plot to keep the notorious resurrection men out. In the 18th century and early 19th century, it was illegal for surgeons to procure corpses for dissection unless they were that of a condemned criminal, for which dissection was a part of their sentence. Dissection was looked upon with such horror that only the worst criminals received it as their punishment. This meant that medical students were denied a vital part of their education, but where there is a demand, there is a supply. Enter the resurrection men, those who dug up bodies of the recently dead to offer them to medical schools at a price. Only the thick iron bars of the mortsafes could keep them at bay.

The Kirkyard appears to have been built on a hill, but that's not exactly true. Back in the 16th century, the place was a shallow depression, but so many people were buried there in the ensuing

400 years that the depression filled up, slowly rising up to form the hill found there today. No one knows how many souls are buried there, but estimates rise to half a million. Most are rather shallow graves, and those who visit after one of Edinburgh's frequent heavy rains might see the white gleam of a bone sticking out of the dark soil.

Visitors peeking through the iron fence at night or strolling through the Kirkyard in the broad daylight have seen white figures floating between the tombstones, and they have heard faint moans and children's laughter coming from nowhere. The worst hauntings—such as the attacks—are centered around the Mackenzie mausoleum, but paranormal phenomena can occur even at the opposite end of the extensive burial ground.

The old neighborhoods of central Edinburgh are a labyrinth of narrow streets and alleys called "closes." In the days before street lighting, all sorts of nefarious activities took place in their dark confines, so it is no wonder that many an old close is home to its own particular ghost. One of these is Brodie's Close, just off the Royal Mile, Edinburgh's main street, leading up to the famous castle. William "Deacon" Brodie was a well-respected town council member in the 18th century who worked as a cabinetmaker and locksmith. He was considered one of the most trustworthy men of his day, and no one hesitated to allow him to work on the front doors of their houses, which proved to be a mistake because he lived a double life as a thief. When he installed a new lock for someone, he always made a duplicate key. Then, he'd bide his time in order to allay any suspicions before sneaking into the home when he knew the residents were away and helping himself to whatever he liked. Brodie wouldn't have needed the money if he lived an honest life—his profession was a successful one—but he was an avid gambler and kept two mistresses with whom he had five children.

Brodie was eventually caught, as most thieves are, and hanged in 1788 in front of a huge crowd, said to have numbered 40,000. The 1791 census counted only 82,706 people in the entire city, so it was obviously a big day. This gawping crowd wasn't the last to see him, because now his ghost wanders up and down Brodie's Close at night, rattling a large ring of keys.

Many other landmarks in town are haunted, too. One of the most notorious is the Learmonth Hotel, a 19th century building with an abundance of poltergeist activity. Unlike ghosts who are seen, heard, and sometimes felt, poltergeists are unseen spirits who move objects. The word comes from the German *poltern* ("to make noise") and *Geist* ("ghost" or "spirit"), and that's exactly what the poltergeists at the Learmonth Hotel do. Doors open and shut by themselves, and sometimes the guests get locked out of their rooms so the spirits can play inside, turning on electrical appliances and whistling strange tunes. Staffers have become resigned to the paranormal goings-on and try to reassure the guests that poltergeists rarely actually hurt anyone.

Then there is Edinburgh's fabled underground warren of tunnels and rooms, called the Vaults. These are a series of corridors and connected, vaulted rooms that run under the city, and have been there for at least two hundred years, perhaps longer. Nobody is all that sure, but it appears that, as is the case with the Paris catacombs, they have been added to over the years. The main line of vaults are actually a series of 19 subterranean arches holding up the city's South Bridge, finished in 1788, but the subterranean passageways extend further than that. Some rooms have been sealed off and converted into pubs and underground nightclubs. Others sit empty.

Kjetil Bjørnsrud's pictures of parts of the Vaults

They were not always so. In the 18th and 19th centuries, there were a large number of indigent rural folk who came to Edinburgh, hoping to find a means of making a living, and ended up sleeping in the Vaults for lack of a better shelter. It was cold, it was damp, and it was pitch dark, but at least it was free.

It was also dangerous. Thieves, murderers, and body snatchers prowled the darkness, and many times the poor residents of the Vaults were awoken by pitiful screams of hapless victims. It is said that many of these victims still lurk in the Vaults today, tied to the place where they suffered in life. It is certainly a disconcerting place. The author visited the Vaults one night with a guide and found them cold and clammy, with strange sounds echoing off the stone walls. Since the Vaults run under inhabited buildings and busy roads, sounds get captured and rebound off the stone, intermingling in strange, eerie ways. It is easy to imagine such a place to be haunted.

One room has been converted into the worship center of a local coven of witches. These are not the witches of fable, but modern practitioners of Wicca, a recognized religion that attempts to recreate and preserve the old folk religion of Europe. Some of the 21st century witches had to cast many purification spells against hostile sprits to cleanse their worship area before they could practice their craft in peace, but the witches were only able to clean out their own vault. Others are still the lairs of angry spirits who appear faintly to living visitors, or whose footsteps still echo down the passageways.

Some of the ghosts are said to be the victims of William Burke and William Hare, the two most notorious resurrection men in Scottish history. In the early 19th century, the law made it extremely difficult for surgeons to procure corpses for dissection, so medical students were denied a vital part of their education. To compensate for this, resurrection men dug up the bodies of the recently dead and offered them to medical schools at a price.

Hare and Burke

Burke and Hare were two Irish immigrants who'd worked various jobs before hitting upon this grim mode of making a living. It is unknown how they ended up as friends, but at some point, Burke moved into Hare's home, where he let out spare rooms to lodgers, and the two made an unlikely partnership. Hare was described, by all contemporary accounts, as a drunken brawler, and a brute. Burke was more educated and professed to be a religious man, although he, too, drank to excess.

Both turned out to be cold-blooded killers. Their first crime came by a stroke of luck, as a contemporary broadside recounts: "In December 1827, a man died in Hare's house, whose body they sold to the Anatomists for £10. Getting so much money at a time when they were in a state of poverty, prompted them to look after means of the same kind, and the subject of murder was often talked over betwixt Hare and [Burke]. The first victim was an old woman belonging to Gilmerton, whom Hare had observed intoxicated on the street, and enticed into his house; they stupified her with more whisky, and put her to death in the way they pursued ever afterwards, by covering and pressing upon the nose and mouth with their hands. The body was carried to Surgeon's Square, and the money readily obtained for it."

The two men justified the sale of the body with the fact that the tenant had owed Hare £4. They had no justification for their second victim, another lodger, whom they got drunk and then suffocated.

In total they were charged with murdering 16 people, all of whom were sold to Dr. Robert Knox, a surgeon who used to lecture on human anatomy by dissecting corpses in front of a paying audience. The bodies were delivered in a large tea chest, the two men acting like they were workers with a delivery for the Surgeons' Hall. Many of the victims were lured into Hare's boarding house, given plenty of liquor, and then strangled. One of the victims was a mentally disabled teenage boy.

The two resurrection men also did away with an old woman and her 12 year-old mute grandson. While Hare smothered the old woman, Burke bent the child over his knee and broke his back. Later, while awaiting execution in prison, Burke confessed that this killing troubled him the most of all his crimes, and that he couldn't get the boy's dying expression out of his head. The tea chest they usually used to deliver the victims proved to be too small to fit both bodies, so they used a herring barrel instead. The two resurrection men put it on a cart drawn by Hare's horse, but when the animal wouldn't pull the heavy load up the steep hill to the Surgeons' Hall, they had to hire a third man—who was unaware of the barrel's grisly contents—to help them move it. Once Hare returned home, he was so infuriated with his horse that he shot it.

Burke and Hare generally had to get drunk to get up the courage to commit their crimes. At his trial, Burke confessed that he "could not sleep at night without a bottle of whisky by his bedside, and a twopenny candle to burn all night beside him; when he awoke he would take a draught of the bottle—sometimes half a bottle at a draught—and that would make him sleep." Clearly, his troubled conscience didn't stop him from committing more murders.

That such a series of killings, all in the space of a single year, should go undetected is testament to the misery in which Edinburgh's poor had to live. The victims were mostly indigent, or poor and working jobs such as junk collectors, and the authorities simply didn't care about them. The killings were almost exposed when the body of the mentally disabled young man was delivered to Dr. Knox. Several of the students recognized him because he was a common and well-known figure who'd wandered the streets, but Knox denied it was him and quickly began the dissection, soon making the corpse unrecognizable. The students made no more fuss about the matter.

Dr. Knox

As Sir Walter Scott would later quip, "Our Irish importation have made a great discovery of Oeconomicks, namely, that a wretch who is not worth a farthing while alive, becomes a valuable article when knockd on the head & carried to an anatomist; and acting on this principle, have cleard the streets of some of those miserable offcasts of society, whom nobody missed because nobody wishd to see them again."

The pair only got caught because a pair of Hare's lodgers, who had somehow survived up to this point, stumbled upon one of the murder victims before Burke and Hare could move the body. By the time the police arrived, they had delivered the body to Knox, but they soon broke down under questioning. It wasn't long before both of them were up before a judge.

The court was faced with a problem, however. They did not have firm evidence for any of the killings except the last, and there was no evidence the final victim had died by violence. The court decided to offer Hare to turn King's evidence, making him free from prosecution if he fingered Burke. This he did, and Burke was found guilty, sentenced to hang, and then have his body publicly dissected.

As one broadside dating to 1829 covering the hanging of William Burke gleefully reported, "His struggles were long and violent, and his body was agonizingly convulsed. We observed that his fall was unusually short, scarcely more than three inches, the noose instead of being as is usual, immediately behind his ear, was at the very summit of the vertebrae. We should have mentioned that when the rope was placed about his neck there was a universal cry raised of 'Burke him;' and, during the whole of the horrible process, there were repeated crys of Hare, Hare. A precentor or clerk was upon the scaffold, as it had been arranged that he should exercise his function; but such were the indications of the feelings of the populace, that those in authority saw it prudent to dispense with this part of the ceremony. Great attempts were made by the Magistrates, officers and others in attendance, upon the scaffold, by signals, to silence the mob during the putting up of prayers; but their efforts were altogether ineffectual. At every struggle the wretch made when suspended, a most rapturous shout was raised by the multitude. When the body was cut down, at three quarters past eight, the most frightful yell we ever heard was raised by the indignant populace, who manifested the most eager desire to get the monster's carcase within their clutches, to gratify their revenge, even after the law had been satisfied, by tearing it to pieces. They were only restrained by the bold front presented by the police. We observed the persons under the scaffold, with knives and scissors, possessing themselves of part of the rope and even slipping into their pockets some of the shavings from the coffin. The scramble at this time was of the most extraordinary nature ever witnessed at an execution in this country."

An illustration of Burke's execution

The surgeon who performed the dissection was Professor Alexander Monro, who, ironically enough, was the man Burke and Hare had originally intended to sell their first victim to. By chance, Munro wasn't around when they delivered the body, and so they ended up selling it to Knox. During the dissection, which attracted record crowds, Monro dipped a quill pen into the dead man's blood and wrote "This is written with the blood of Wm Burke, who was hanged at Edinburgh. This blood was taken from his head."

Burke's skull was given to the Edinburgh Phrenological Society for study. Phrenology is a quack medical belief that was popular at that time. It proposed the theory that a person's character and intellect could be perceived by studying the bumps on his head. Burke must have had some fascinating bumps. The residents of Edinburgh were fascinated by his skin too, and they cut it up, tanned it into leather, and used it to make wallets.

Modern visitors can still see relics from this horrible chapter in Edinburgh's history. Burke's skeleton is on display at the Anatomical Museum of the Edinburgh Medical School. The phrenologists eventually tired of fondling the murderer's skull and reunited it with the skeleton for the sake of posterity. Over at the museum housed in Old Surgeons' Hall, yoneou can see his death mask, and a book supposedly bound in his tanned skin. Some of Knox's surgical instruments are also on display. While the Burke skin wallets have all disappeared, a calling card case made from the skin of the back of his left hand is on display at the Cadies & Witchery Tours museum.

Kim Traynor's picture of Old Surgeons' Hall

Despite Burke's inglorious end, his victims have not been able to rest. Locals whisper that some of the screams that can be heard echoing through the Vaults at night are those of the poor people the two men murdered. Others hear the rumble of the resurrection men's cart in the street outside the Old Surgeons' Hall. Perhaps the spirits are restless because Hare got off "Scot-free," and Knox also escaped prosecution because Burke insisted throughout the trial that the surgeon did not know the bodies were those of murder victims. Even the passage of the Anatomy Act of 1832, which made it easier to obtain cadavers for dissection, and which was a direct result of the Burke and Hare murders, did not lay the spirits to rest. To this day they call for justice from beyond the grave.

Haunted Pubs and Churches

Parapsychologists say that ghosts are often tied to places that were important to them in life. Someone who suffered a violent death may linger in the spot where he met his end, while others may continue to pass down a road they frequented while they were still among the living. Thus, it is not surprising that many ghosts haunt two places important to most Scots: the church and the pub. Both are places where people seek solace, and both are often old buildings that have seen their share of history.

Some of them even keep their dead residents after falling into ruin. One such building is St. Andrew's Cathedral, founded in the 12th century. As is the case with many of Europe's great cathedrals, it took generations to build and was dedicated in 1318 in a ceremony attended by Robert the Bruce. Soon, pilgrims from all over the land were coming to St. Andrew's to hear the sermons and pray for miracles from Scotland's patron saint. Several relics from St. Andrew himself were housed in the cathedral, including one of his teeth, an arm bone, a kneecap, and three fingers. The magnificent 12th century building was actually built atop a much older church that may date all the way back to 700, well before the land was completely Christianized, and St. Andrew's relics had their home there before receiving a much grander building. The relics drew pilgrims to the site at a time when many believed in their miraculous healing powers.

Like so many fine houses of worship, it fell prey to the Scottish Reformation, during which the country broke with the Catholic Church. In the process, it was stripped of its ornaments in 1559 and abandoned in 1561.

After almost 500 years of neglect, much of the cathedral has vanished, but what remains is stunning in its grandeur. Parts of the wall survive with their original arches, as does the east gable of the presbytery that once housed St. Andrew's relics. These impressive twin towers and connecting arches somehow survived while much of the rest of the building was dismantled and the stones reused for later buildings.

The tallest part of the cathedral is St. Rule's tower, the last remnant of the cathedral's predecessor, St. Rule's Church, built around 1130. The square tower is 33 meters (108 feet) high. The views from the top of it are truly magnificent, with the ruins of the cathedral, the nearby town, and sea all laid out beneath.

Robert de Montrose, a prior of St. Andrews from 1387-1394, enjoyed the view so much, he went up almost every night to get a glimpse, especially when the moon was full. By all accounts, Robert de Montrose was a kindly and fair man, but in his office as prior, he sometimes had to be the disciplinarian. Once, the case of a monk who had committed a number of crimes, including fornication, came before him, and Robert was forced to punish the man severely. The monk took his punishment, but resentment grew within him. One fine, moonlit night, when the goodly prior climbed to the top of the tower, the monk quietly followed him. The prior was too entranced by the view to either see or hear him, and the monk drew a dagger from his pocket, stabbed the prior in the back, and pushed him out the window to fall to his death.

Nevertheless, the prior still sometimes makes the climb to the top of the tower, especially on those clear, moonlit nights he so loved. Visitors have seen him standing at the window, a beatific smile on his lips, while less fortunate witnesses have seen him falling to the ground. Of course, they rush to the spot to help, but they never find a body.

Despite his cruel end, Robert de Montrose has remained just as kindly as ever. An account from 1948 tells how a visitor was climbing the tower when he came to a dark area, unlit by the tower's then-meager lighting. His foot slipped on a worn step, and he had to grab onto the handrail to keep from tumbling down the stone steps and probably getting killed. Just then, he noticed a man wearing a cassock standing on the stairs above him. The clergyman addressed him in a low, pleasant voice, telling him it was all right and that the visitor could hold onto him for safety. The man replied that he was all right now and moved past the figure. Only when he got to the top did he realize he hadn't felt anything when he brushed by the man in the cassock. When he had made it back down and asked the watchman, he learned that no one had been up there but him, and that he must have met old Robert de Montrose.

Another, less personable ghost also supposedly inhabits these ruins. Enclosing the cathedral precinct is a protective wall that once had 16 towers, although a few have now disappeared. One of the survivors is a two-story structure positioned just east of the cathedral's east gable. It is there that nighttime visitors sometimes see the White Lady. She is seen in many places on the property, but when she appears, she is always heading toward the tower, vanishing once she gets there. People describe her as a beautiful woman floating over the ground in a flowing white dress and wearing white leather gloves. She has been seen for at least 200 years, although no one knows who she is.

In 1868, two masons repairing the tower discovered a hidden room containing several coffins, and all of them were closed except for one containing the well-preserved remains of a woman wearing a white dress and white gloves. There were no clues as to why that particular coffin was open. Some theorize that the dead woman had been robbed of her jewelry, while others claim the ghost herself opened it. The coffins were all reburied, but that hasn't stopped the White Lady from appearing now and then, near where her eternal rest had once been disturbed.

Another old house of worship with resident ghosts is Culross Abbey, founded in 1217 on the hallowed spot where Saint Serf built a church in the 6th century to convert pagans. Much of it is now a picturesque ruin, although the eastern section still functions as the parish church. Local legend says there's a secret tunnel running from the abbey for an unknown distance beneath the countryside. Somewhere down there, a spirit sits on a golden chair, waiting to give an immense treasure to whoever finds him.

A blind piper once decided to go in search of the spirit and descended into the tunnel with his dog. He played his pipes to signal his progress to those above, and a curious crowd followed him for nearly a mile before the piping suddenly stopped. Several days later, the dog reappeared, but the piper never returned. Within the abbey grounds, many have seen processions of ghostly monks filing past, intent on their prayers even after they had gone to achieve their eternal reward.

Kim Traynor's picture of the abbey

Many of Scotland's old pubs and wayside inns are haunted as well. One of the most famous is the Drovers Inn in the town of Inverarnan, along the River Falloch, near the head of Loch Lomond. The town and inn have long been a stopping point for travelers looking for a meal, a few pints, and a bed. In the early days, before the old coaching routed, Highland drovers led their herds to the Lowlands for sale. In later years, steamboats passed up and down the loch. Nowadays, it's a popular rest stop for hikers along the West Highland Way, one of Scotland's great trails.

The region acted as a boundary in ancient times. A stone circle stands near the village, and many archaeologists theorize that these circles marked meeting places for different tribes. Nearby stands the Stone of the Britons, a natural outcropping that served as a boundary stone for three kingdoms: Pictland to the east; Dumbarton and Strathclyde to the south; and Dál Riata to the northwest. Thus, it was the meeting point for the Picts, the Britons, and the Scots.

The area has been a focal point for centuries, and such places often act as a magnet for the paranormal. Several spots in the town of Inverarnan and the surrounding countryside are said to be haunted, but most haunted of all is the Drovers Inn, founded in 1705 and named for the many drovers who have found rest and relaxation there over the years.

The oldest ghost to inhabit the inn dates to 1792. Locally known as the "Year of the Sheep," it was the same year many landlords decided that raising sheep was more profitable than parceling out the land to tenant farmers, so they evicted hundreds of families. These people, already poor, lost their sole means of income and were left to fend for themselves in the middle of winter.

One family, a young couple with a little boy, lived a couple of days' walk from the Drovers Inn. They decided to head south to find work, perhaps to the Lowlands or to one of England's cities get a job in one of the new factories. They trudged their weary way down the old drovers' road through the first day and slept in the open that night. On the second day, half-dead from the cold, they knew they had to make it to the Drovers Inn to find shelter or they would surely perish. When a storm blew in, the family became disoriented, never made it to the inn, and froze to death like so many other families that dreadful winter. Now, on cold winter evenings, hikers arriving late at the Drovers Inn sometimes tell of having seem a bedraggled family in old-style clothing struggling through the snow and wind. The family is also seen inside the inn itself. A couple staying in Room Two awoke in the middle of the night, freezing cold. At first, they thought the heating had broken, but then, at the foot of the bed, they saw the sad, little family, shivering in the icy air. The boy waved to them forlornly, and then the sad scene vanished.

Another chilling experience sometimes happens in Room Six. Someone will be sleeping soundly when they suddenly awaken, cold and wet. They open their eyes and are shocked to see a small girl lying next to them, soaking wet and radiating a bone-chilling cold. When the girl vanishes, the room slowly returns to its normal temperature. The startled guest, however, generally doesn't get any more sleep.

The girl is the phantom of a real child who drowned in the River Falloch, just behind the inn. She was playing with her doll after a hard rain in the early part of the century. The river ran high and fast, and the unsupervised child strayed too close to it. She dropped her doll into the water by accident, and when she tried to retrieve it, she was swept away and drowned. Some local men found her, brought back her to the inn, and put her in Room Six until they could summon the authorities. The doll was never recovered, though it is sometimes seen, walking around like a miniature person, searching for the lost little girl who had once loved it so much.

Other ghosts haunt the inn as well, such as the shade of a cattle drover who was murdered by thieves. There are also strange light orbs that flit around the rooms at night. A stay in this inn can definitely come with a bonus experience.

In the town of Kirkcaldy, Fife, about halfway between St. Andrew's and Edinburgh, there are at least two haunted pubs. The Feuars Arms, a well-preserved Victorian pub, is a center of poltergeist activity. People have felt an invisible hand tap them on their shoulders or heard footsteps running up and down the stairs when there is no one there. The beer pumps sometimes turn themselves on or off as well, and the staff report the cellar is unusually cold and forbidding. Back in 2005, a team of paranormal investigators examined the pub, and several witnesses saw a glass slide across a table when no one was touching it.

Betty Nicols, a pub which first appeared in town records in 1741 but is probably older, has been serving drinks for generations. It is now a gastropub, and it has also seen a number of strange events over the years. Once, a cleaning lady came in the early morning to find the pub locked up and deserted, but she found a candle burning at one of the tables. It must have been lit in the wee hours of the morning because it was a small tea light, the kind that only burns for a couple of hours. Curious as to who had created this obvious fire hazard, the owners of the pub reviewed CCTV footage, and, to their astonishment, they saw the candle light up on its own. No one was seen on the tape between closing time and when the cleaner arrived the next morning.

While most ghostly encounters happen late at night when all is quiet, visitors to this pub often experience hauntings when the place is full. The shadowy figures of two men and a dog are sometimes seen crossing the bar. Pay close attention when looking into the mirrors, and some of the people seen in the mirrors might not actually be standing in the room.

Like the Feuars Arms, the cellar in Betty Nicols is cold and disturbing. Many of the staff have complained that they feel as if they are being watched when they do.

Remote Ghosts

Some of the greatest attractions in Scotland are its many wild and remote areas. Millions of visitors enjoy wonderful days hiking across its rugged landscape without seeing another person. Of course, that isn't to say there aren't any souls about; in fact, Scotland's more isolated areas seem to attract ghosts.

Take Cape Wrath, for instance. This rugged spit of land on the extreme northwest coast is one of the most dramatic spots in Scotland, and one of its most remote. The area is made up of jagged sea cliffs and bleak moorland, much of it owned by the Ministry of Defense, so few people go there. The nearest village is ten miles away. There is also a lighthouse at the cape, which is where the ghost resides.

Built in 1828, the lighthouse run automatically since 1998, but a lighthouse keeper manned it before then. During that period, the lighthouse received regular visitors, some who came to supply the keeper as well as some adventuresome hikers wanting to see one of Scotland's most dramatic and remote locations. Many have reported a strange apparition near the ruined cottage not far from the lighthouse. He appears as a tall man, well over 6' tall, wearing a three-cornered hat, knee-length boots, and a long, dark coat. He is seen quite clearly and looks real, unlike the transparent or glowing apparitions witnessed in other locations, but he will vanish if anyone approaches. Local lore says he was the captain of a ship that smashed on the rocks in the 18th century before the lighthouse had been installed. Now, he wanders the spot where he and his crew drowned, keeping an eye on the shipping and making sure the lighthouse remains lit. Some ghost hunters have joked the place would be better called "Cape Wraith." Sightings of the captain have waned in recent years, perhaps because fewer people visit the spot or perhaps because the spirit is simply fading away as spirits sometimes do.

Scotland is fringed with islands, windswept by harsh North Atlantic and North Sea winds and rains that have bred tough, independent people and many local traditions. The Orkney Islands, 10 miles (16 kilometers) off the north coast of Scotland, are the most hospitable, with a relatively mild if wet climate and a population of more than 20,000 on its approximately 70 islands. There is a great deal of debate in local pubs as to what constitutes an island, as opposed to nothing more than a rock sticking out from the sea. These rocks are often called skerries, but the dividing line between skerry and island is not altogether clear. A general definition for a skerry is that it is too small to be inhabited, but even that doesn't settle the debate. For example, there's a rock in the harbor of Kirkwall, the islands' capital, about the size of a large living room. It has a bit of grass on it and not much else. Could this be classified as a skerry? Some may say so, as the rock was inhabited at times, used as a prison for unfortunate Norsemen who were marooned there in plain view of the mainland. Needless to say, they didn't survive long.

This rock does not appear to harbor any ghosts, but many spots in the Orkney Islands do. Many of them are those of young children, unfortunate enough to have died before being baptized. This was a frequent occurrence in the more remote islands because of the lack of priests. Some children waited years before being baptized as a result.

Two children on the island of North Ronaldsay suffered such a fate. At some time in the early 19th century, they both died from an illness and were buried in the garden by their bereaved parents. Thus, not only did they die unbaptized, they were denied a Christian burial. The garden stood by a lane, and passersby often report a feeling of dread coming from the place. At dusk, strange, white birds fly straight up into the sky. At night, eerie lights bob around the enclosure. Things got so bad that the locals investigated, found the remains of the two children, and gave them a proper burial in the island's little churchyard. Though no one feels a sense of uncanny fear while passing the churchyard these days, nor do they see white birds, the strange lights still make an occasional appearance. Perhaps they are the spirits of the children, wondering where their home had gone.

Clearly, a Christian burial is no guarantee of a peaceful spirit if the dead are disturbed. Such was the case of Baubie Skithawa on the island of Sanday.

Baubie Skithawa was an old woman who had led what passed for a prosperous life on the islands. She had a good farmstead, plenty to eat, and clothes on her back. When she was dying, she made her final purchase: a set of new clothes and a winding-sheet of fine material she found at the Lammas Fair in Kirkwall, the capital of Orkney. Old Baubie had always taken good care of her appearance, and she wanted to look good in the afterlife, too.

When the time came for her to pass on, the local midwife laid her out for her wake, dressed her in her final outfit, and wrapped her in her fine winding-sheet. All her neighbors came by to pay their respects, including one strange old recluse everyone called "Black Jock" because her ancestors supposedly made a deal with the Devil to cast black magic. Since everyone feared her, no one dared object to her presence. As everyone sat the night through with the body, a custom that is now rarely honored, she was heard several times to have muttered what a pity it was that such nice clothing and such a nice winding-sheet should be buried.

After the proper observances, Baubie Skithawa was buried in the graveyard at Cross Kirk. A couple of days later, Black Jock snuck into the cemetery, dug the body up, stripped it naked, and stole the clothing and winding-sheet for herself. She took these items home and hid them.

Black Jock covered her tracks well. She had been getting up to all sorts of mischief throughout her life, and she knew how to hide her crimes. Black Jock placed the sod back onto the grave so expertly that the gravedigger himself wouldn't have noticed that the plot had been disturbed, but the dead have their own ways of warning the living. The day after poor old Baubie's grave was desecrated, a young man named Andrew Moodie walked past the graveyard at dusk and saw the most frightening sight of his life. The sky turned suddenly black, the clouds roiled, and lightning flashed. Pillars of fire shot from the churchyard, rising high into the sky. At the top of each pillar hovered the spirits of the dead, waving their arms, their grave clothes and winding-sheets fluttering in the hard wind, beckoning to each other as if to attract the other's attention. They gestured to one pillar, in particular, seeming to laugh and mock the spirit floating atop it. Andrew Moodie quickly saw why - it was the spirit of Baubie Skithawa, stark naked in the fiery night, wailing with shame and anger as she tried to cover her nakedness.

Needless to say, Andrew Moodie fled from that place as fast as his feet would carry him to the nearest cottage, which happened to be that of Black Jock. There, he pounded on the door, begging to be let in. At first, Black Jock refused him entry, but he put up such a racket that she finally relented. Young Andrew shot into the cottage as soon as the door opened. Black Jock slammed it shut behind him, barring it with a wooden yoke into which she stuck three iron awls. Iron, of course, is a sure charm against spirits. Andrew felt a bit safer upon seeing this, although, like everyone else on Sanday, he steered clear of Black Jock under normal circumstances.

The storm still raged outside, and Black Jock raged at her unwelcome guest. She told him to sit in a corner and keep his mouth shut. Then, as the thunder banged and the lightning flashed, Black Jock took pieces of sod and stuffed every hole in the house—the window, the smoke hole, even the cat hole above the door, an old feature of traditional Orcadian architecture. Then she sat in the center of the room, picked up a needle, and drew circles around herself on the dirt floor.

Outside, the storm grew in intensity, and Andrew heard another sound besides the wind, thunder, and lightning. It sounded like the cries of a host of people, wailing and speaking all at once. One by one, the pieces of sod that stopped up the holes in the house were pushed out, and ghostly hands reached inside. Andrew cowered in the corner of the room as Black Jock continued her incantations, her face a mask of terror.

Then Baubie Skithawa's pale face appeared at the window. "Give me back my grave clothes!" she cried. "Give me back my winding-sheet! I am cold! I am colder than death! Oh, what a torture it is to be shameful and naked in the cold, wet earth. Give them back to me!" A ghostly arm reached through the cat hole and down to the bolt barring the door. The phantom hand touched one of the iron awls that had been driven into the bolt and recoiled, for no spirit can touch iron. The ghosts wailed in frustration. Andrew realized that it was near dawn and the ghosts would soon have to return from whence they came.

The spirit of Baubie Skithawa screamed at the window and then stretched forth, elongating unnaturally and reaching its head and arms into the room. The ghostly hands tried to grab Black Jock but were repelled by the magic circle the witch had drawn around herself. Then they reached for Andrew where he was cowering in the corner and slapped him on the top of the head. The force of the blow knocked him down, and as he fell, his foot scraped over the circle in the dirt floor, breaking the magic and knocking the needle out of Black Jock's hand. The witch knew the game was up, and she raced to her chest by the foot of her bed, flung it open, and pulled out the stolen winding-sheet and grave clothing. As soon as she did, they flew out of her hands and straight out the window. With a cry of victory, the spirits withdrew. Then, an invisible force smacked into Black Jock and laid her flat on the floor.

To his profound relief, Andrew heard the cockcrow. The storm abated, no more wails came from without, and all grew calm. But all was not well. His head stung from the blow he had received, and when he reached up to rub it, he discovered a bald spot in the shape of a palm and five fingers. No hair would ever grow there again.

Black Jock was worse off. She lay where she had been knocked down, and when Andrew tried to pull her up, he found no amount of force would budge her. The young man ran for help, telling all the neighbors of the terrible things he had witnessed. They, too, tried to pull Black Jock up, but with no success, so they summoned Mansie Peace, a local cunning man who had a great amount of experience in such matters. He walked around her prone body seven times, chanting seven prayers. Then, he boiled seven bluestones in water, allowed the water to cool, and poured the water over Black Jock. She was finally able to rise, and when she got to her feet, she was a changed woman. Never again did she pester her neighbors with magic, and never again did the graveyard at Cross Kirk have a ghostly apparition. Andrew Moodie, however, bore the mark of the ghostly hand on his scalp for the rest of his days.

The Shetland Islands are even more remote than Orkney. This archipelago of some 300 islands and skerries can be found 50 miles (80 kilometers) to the northeast of Orkney, blasted by Atlantic and North Sea storms. The islands are ringed with jagged cliffs and made up of low, rolling hills. Few trees grow there, and its industry is limited mostly to sheepherding, a bit of crofting, and fishing. There are also extensive oil and natural gas fields in the surrounding waters. The winters are harsh, and the summers short, but the Shetlanders love their islands and are proud of their traditions, but they're probably a little less proud having one of the most haunted houses in Britain.

Windhouse is the ruined home of a laird ("lord") that dates to the early 18th century. It sits on a hill by the settlement of Mid Yell, on the island of Yell, the second largest island in the archipelago besides Mainland. The Windhouse hasn't been inhabited since the 1930s and is now an empty ruin with little more than its walls still standing. True to its name, the hard sea wind howls through the empty corridors and glassless windows, creating an eerie feeling.

Even when it was in use, it was haunted. Residents complained of several different spirits waking them up from their sleep and flitting through the hallways. One such tale associated with the place is called "The Trow of Windhouse" and dates to the early 19th century. A "trow" is the local word for fairy folk, who come in various forms, as this tale shows.

One day, a sailor was shipwrecked on the shore nearby Yell, and he was the only survivor of the wreck. Having sunk in such a remote spot, no one came to help him. He managed to wade ashore, carrying a steel ax. He didn't know how or why he had grabbed it from the wreck, especially since it certainly hadn't helped him swim, but he had the feeling he might need it. The soaked sailor wandered around the bleak hills for a time until he saw Windhouse. He hurried to knock on the door to beg for help, and the laird and his family were kind enough to bring him in and let him warm by the fire. They also gave him some tea and food. The family was busy packing, however, and told the sailor that if he knew what was good for him, he'd leave with them. It was Christmas Eve, the family told him, and that date was always one of woe for the family, for every year a trow would visit them and carry one of them off.

The sailor was tired after his ordeal and didn't fear anything of this world or the next, so he opted to stay. The family shrugged their shoulders and cleared out. That night, the sailor discovered the family had spoken the truth when a huge, shapeless mass came up to the house. The hardy sailor showed no fear, and it only took one swipe of his trusty ax to fell the beast. The next morning was Christmas Day, the family returned, and the sailor told his tale. When he took them out to show where he had killed the trow, the body had disappeared. All that remained was a patch of heather—colored a bright green—that had grown higher than the surrounding plants. Locals still point out this patch of heather as proof of the story.

Locals say the dark forces associated with the site came from the fact the Windhouse had been built on a graveyard. There were gravestones found during construction, and the cemetery wasn't marked on any map, but everyone on the island firmly believed this to be true.

The ghosts haven't left. To this day, some visitors have spotted an elegant woman dressed in silk, supposedly the mistress of the house from a long-ago generation who met her end when she fell down the stairs and broke her neck. It is claimed that her skeleton was found beneath the main staircase at a later time. Why she was buried there rather than in the graveyard is unclear. Others say she was murdered.

A different staircase attracts the more humble ghost of a servant girl who walks up the steps even though the stairs themselves have long since rotted away. There's even the spirit of a dog who approaches brave hikers who venture to the spot. It seems friendly enough, but when the visitors try to pet it, the dog vanishes into thin air. Other manifestations include strange noises, shadows through which no light penetrates, dark figures who walk through walls, and feelings of dread in certain rooms. One bedroom produced such a feeling of fear in all who entered that no one would sleep there. A maid who worked at the house for many years refused to even make the bed because every time she attempted to do so, a booming laugh resonated throughout the room.

Residents have also reported cold breezes coming from nowhere, even when the windows were closed, and some rooms suddenly becoming ice cold. This is a common occurrence in haunted places. Ghost hunters theorize that when spirits try to manifest, they draw ambient energy from the surrounding air, causing the temperature to plummet.

On one occasion in the early 20th century, the family that lived there went for a walk and didn't return until after sunset. As they approached the dark house, the windows lit up one after the other until the entire house was ablaze with light, despite the fact the house had no electricity at the time. As the family stood there in utter shock, the lights went out one by one, as mysteriously as they had appeared.

Remarkably, in 2017, archaeologists discovered two skeletons on the site, confirming the long-held belief that Windhouse stood on a burial ground. Judging from artifacts found with the mortal remains, the cemetery dated to the 13th or 14th century, long before the house had been built. The graves were shallow, with only six inches of soil above them, no doubt because the soil layer in many areas of the rocky island is quite thin.

The excavations were done in preparation for the restoration of the house, which still continues. The team is convinced they will find more burials in the future. Perhaps their discoveries will help to finally lay the old spirits to rest.

The west coast of Scotland is fringed with hundreds of rocky islands, some small skerries, others major pieces of land. The largest island group is the Outer Hebrides, also known as the Western Isles, off the northwest coast. 15 of these islands are inhabited, while more than 50 others are not. Even the shortest visit to one of them will explain why, as the rugged, rocky hills are hard to build on and don't offer much soil for farming or grazing. They do, however, offer some of the most breathtaking scenery in all of the British Isles, so hardy travelers have their efforts richly rewarded.

One of the most popular destinations is also one of the kindest: the Isle Of Lewis. This is a misnomer since it's actually the northern part of the Isle of Lewis and Harris. Lewis is the flatter part, with the largest concentration of population in all the Outer Hebrides, as well as its biggest settlement, Stornoway. Stornoway has a population of more than 8,000, while Harris is mountainous and sparsely populated. They are so different that they might as well be different islands, and they are often referred to as such. The islanders' traditional lifestyle, arts and crafts, and the area's natural beauty attract a steady trickle of visitors.

One place they do not generally go except to zip along the road from Stornoway to Harris is Arnish Moor, a bleak, open wetland. It was on these moors more than three centuries ago that tragedy struck. Back around the year 1700, two boys decided to skip school and go out on Arnish Moor to collect grouse eggs, which make for a very tasty breakfast. After a few hours, they decided to go home, but they argued over who should get which number of eggs. One boy said he had collected more, while the other vehemently disagreed. The first boy got so incensed that he picked up a large stone and smacked his friend over the head with it. He probably meant only to hurt his friend, but the boy didn't know his own strength and caved the other boy's skull in. Panicked, the young murderer hid the body, ran off to the nearest port, and jumped on a ship to become a sailor.

The boy spent several years at sea, but he was an islander, born and bred, and he longed to see his home again. Eventually, he returned, having grown and changed so much that no one recognized him. He checked into a local inn at the edge of the moor and asked for supper. The landlady served his meal, giving him cutlery with unusual bone handles. When he commented on them, she replied that she had found a collection of sheep's bones buried out on the moor. The sailor's eyes grew wide. Had they truly been sheep's bones, or were they something more sinister? Not wanting to draw suspicion to himself, he tried to act casual and picked up the cutlery, even though he had lost his appetite.

While he tried to eat his meal, he felt something wet on his hands. When he looked down, he saw the bone handles of his knife and fork were oozing blood. There's an old Scottish saying that a murdered body will bleed if the murderer touches it, and in this case, it turned out to be true. The sailor went almost mad with fright and immediately confessed his old crime. The judge ordered him to be hanged.

Sadly, the murdered boy was never laid to rest. The landlady couldn't remember the exact spot where she had found the bones and thus couldn't give the complete skeleton a Christian burial, except for the grisly cutlery. Now, the boy wanders the moor, occasionally chasing motorists on the lonely stretch of road near where he was murdered. One motorcyclist swore he was speeding down the road and was chased by the shade of the boy for several miles.

In 1964, a much-decayed body was found half-buried on the moor, dressed in clothing typical of the late 17th century. When archaeologists examined the young male, they found he had died from a blow to the back of the head with a blunt, hard object. Was this the body of the young collector of grouse eggs uncovered at last? The body was identified as that of a man, aged between 20 and 25, which is too old to fit the story, and there were no missing bones.

Perhaps there are more bodies on the moor waiting to be found.

Early Irish Hauntings

According to the local legends, Ireland has been haunted since prehistoric times. The Celts lived in a world where spirits mingled with the living, where warriors displayed the heads of their defeated victims and one night a year the border between the land of the living and the land of the dead would break down.

That night was called Samhain, which people now know as Halloween. It was the dividing line between the light part of the year (spring and summer) and the dark part of the year (autumn and winter). People all over Celtic Ireland would gather for large bonfires. All the hearths at home would be extinguished, and everyone would meet their neighbors at the bonfires for a big feast. Since ghosts and other supernatural creatures were abroad on this night, the people would dress as monsters to blend in and not be bothered. At the feast, people would give food to those less fortunate than they. Once the festivities were over, each household would take a flame from the communal bonfire to bring home with them to relight the hearth for the new year.

A painting of one such celebration in Ireland in 1833

This all had important symbolic value. The communal fire acted as a counterbalance to the darkening of the world, and the communal feast was a way to bring good cheer and tuck in a bit of fat on your belly to get you through the lean months to come. Bringing some of the fire home with you brought good fortune to the home, and strengthened the sense of community.

How the Celts carried the flame home created another enduring Halloween tradition. They would carve out a turnip or beet and place a bit of charcoal and kindling inside. Turnips were favored for being more durable. This became known as the Jack-o'-Lantern. Pumpkins are a New World crop and weren't available in the supermarkets until recently, so turnips and beets were used all over Ireland. One can still see carved turnips in Ireland's various folklore museums, and they make a scary sight with their deformed, grinning faces.

An Irish turnip lantern

Not all the dead were frightening or dangerous. Families would welcome the spirits of loved ones into the home although they had to be treated with care. Something would be left for them such as a dram of whiskey or a bit of food. This developed into the tradition of "trick or treat," where children of the neighborhood would go from house to house dressed as ghosts and ask for treats (often in those days a bit of buttered bread or a half penny). If they didn't get enough, they'd play some prank on the house. This symbolized the spirit that used to live there coming home and expecting to be appeased. If it came away unsatisfied, there might be a bit of haunting that year.

It's important to remember the original purpose of Samhain. While now it's mostly a commercialized party, even today some folks in Ireland, and those of Irish descent, will keep a candle burning all night long next to the photos of those they miss, and will sit up until dawn in vigil. It's a lovely way to remember the dead even for those who are not religious.

Various stories have cropped up about Halloween or Samhain over the years. The Irish don't all follow the folkloric or historical explanation for the Jack-o'-Lantern's origins. Some say

Ireland developed the tradition of Jack-o'-Lanterns because of the deeds of a certain blacksmith who lived many, many years ago named Jack. He was a dishonest man and a clever one. Once Jack managed to trap the Devil by fooling him into turning into a coin in order that they might buy something. Jack decided to keep the coin and put it in his pocket along with a crucifix. Of course the Devil was powerless next to the holy symbol and couldn't change back to his true form.

Eventually Jack freed him with the promise not to put him into Hell, a place Jack was sure to go for his many dishonest dealings. That didn't stop the Dark Lord from haunting his house or sending his minions to harry him, so on another occasion Jack tricked the Devil into climbing a tree to get some fruit. Once he was up there, Jack carved a cross on the trunk and would only let the Devil down on the promise not to bother him for ten years.

When Jack eventually died, Heaven refused to take him and Hell couldn't take him either thanks to the Devil's promise, so now Jack is doomed to walk the Earth for all eternity. The Devil, being the generous sort, gave him a bit of a fire in a turnip to light his way at night. He's been called Jack of the Lantern, or Jack-o'-Lantern, ever since. Sometimes on lonely stretches of road, people still see him, his carved turnip casting a feeble light to guide his weary feet.

Another survival from Celtic times is the legend of the banshee. This is a female spirit that can be heard wailing sorrowfully at night. Her origins are lost to time and now the Irish have two different explanations for why she haunts Ireland's lonely places. One is that she is the ghost of a woman who lost her children before she herself died. The other explanation for the banshee is that it is a fairy coming to mourn humans who have died, often but not necessarily children, or to warn a family that they would soon suffer a loss. The term banshee comes from the Irish *bean sidhe*, meaning "woman of the fairies," giving support to the second theory although many local tales lend credence to the first. Certain aristocratic families often had their own banshee who would wail outside their home or castle when a family member was about to die.

The banshee is found in even the earliest Irish texts. In the eighth century prose tale *Táin Bó Fraích*, "The Raid of Fraích's Cattle") which tells of the heroic exploits of Fraoch mac Idath, the hero's death is foretold by the cries of various women from the Otherworld.

Descriptions of the banshee vary. Sometimes she's a short, old crone with flowing white hair. This type of banshee is usually the one attached to a family as a harbinger of doom. Banshees that are young and tall and beautiful are usually those who have lost their children. Both types go bareheaded and wear a white cloak.

One story of a banshee comes from County Galway, where she was seen on the eve of the Battle of Aughrim in 1691, the decisive battle of the Williamite War, where thousands of Irishmen lost their lives. It was one of the bloodiest ever fought on Irish soil and crushed the Jacobite cause in Ireland. English author John Dunton wrote of this battle the next year in his book *Teague Land*: "After the battle the English did not tarry to bury any of the dead but their own, and left those of the enemy exposed to the fowls of the air, for the country was then so uninhabited that there were not hands to inter them. Many dogs resorted to this aceldama where for want of other food they fed on man's flesh, and thereby became so dangerous and fierce that a single person could not pass that way without manifest hazard."

On the day before the battle, Sir Burke, the Earl of Clanricarde, and a servant were riding to join their army when they came to a ford in a stream. There they saw an old crone washing bloodstained clothes. Thinking they had missed the fight, they asked whose clothes they were. She replied in a keening voice, "They are yours, Sir Burke, and those of your servant and many more besides." The next day both men were killed in battle.

A tale from County Wexford shows that the banshee wasn't without a certain grim sense of humor. In Wexford Town the local banshee is referred to as "The Bow" and has a habit of dropping her combs. Everyone in Wexford Town knows not to pick up a comb that they find lying on the ground because it belongs to "The Bow" and she's sure to come back for it. But there was a local drunk (as there often is in these stories) who claimed he wasn't afraid of the banshee. Instead of picking up a comb on the street, he decided to go one better. Stumbling home late one night after the last pub closed, he came across "The Bow," wailing as she floated along the lane and holding a comb in her hand. The drunk decided to show off by snatching the comb from her. He did manage to get the comb, but the banshee had the last laugh. She threw a curse on him.

Before he knew what was going on, an invisible force lifted him up and put him on a windowsill on the upper story of a nearby building, still holding the comb. He was told he would have to stay there for 48 hours as punishment. He also found that the comb had become stuck to his hand and he couldn't drop it. Soon other drunks staggering home spotted his predicament and called the fire brigade, who arrived and sent up a ladder to bring him down. To their shock, they found an invisible barrier between them and the drunk. He was left up there for the duration of the curse, the object of public derision and a sign of what would happen if you crossed "The Bow." Perhaps the man's worst punishment was that he didn't get to have a drink for two whole days.

In Shane's Castle on the shores of Lough Neah in Antrim, there's a room reserved for a banshee. She is said to appear regularly, sometimes hooded and hard to see, sometimes looking like a beautiful but mournful young maiden. Family tradition states that the banshee is actually the spirit of a member of the castle's hereditary family, the O'Neills. It was a girl named Kathleen, who was taken away by the fairy folk, only allowed to return when a member of the family was about to die.

Kenneth Allen's picture of the ruins of Shane's Castle

Another female spirit is the fearsome Demon Bride. This baleful ghost has haunted the Errigal-Truagh Graveyard in County Monaghan for more than two centuries. It waits until there is a funeral in the graveyard, watching the mourners carefully. As the grieving family and friends file out of the cemetery, one person will often linger for a moment. If this final mourner is a young man, the Demon Bride appears as a beautiful young woman and chats with the fellow, whose sadness turns to interest at the attentions of the comely stranger. The Demon Bride tells the young man how handsome he is and how much she fancies him. At this point, she gets him to promise to return to the cemetery exactly one month later, in order to get "better acquainted." They seal the promise with a kiss, a kiss so passionate that the man is fired with lust.

At that point the lady vanishes. The young man blinks in surprise, not sure what has happened. As he staggers out of the graveyard, he remembers the local tale of the Demon Bride, and realizes he's lost his soul to a spirit from the other side, which makes him go mad, his raving terror destroying his health until he dies. Exactly one month after he's met the Demon Bride, he keeps his promise by being buried in the Errigal-Truagh Graveyard.

Ireland's Haunted Castles

Ireland has seen much conflict in its long history and is home to numerous castles. Some have become stately homes or even hotels, while others became victims of war or time and have now become atmospheric ruins.

Antrim Castle in County Antrim, for example, is haunted by the ghost of a servant girl. Unusually for ghosts, people even know her real name and there is proof that she existed.

A contemporary sketch of Antrim Castle

The 17th century castle was first used as a fortified home by the Clotworthys, a leading Anglo-Irish family, but was transformed into a more luxurious home in the early 1800s. This was common after castles lost their defensive value in an age of widespread use of artillery. The house prospered for many years and was notable for its fine Italianate architecture and spacious gardens laid out in the French style. On October 28, 1922, however, tragedy struck; during a grand ball that brought in many leading members of the community, a fire broke out and quickly raged through the old building. The speed and extent of the fire made many suspect that the Irish Republican Army had a hand in it, and the Clotworthys were certainly unpopular with the IRA thanks to their ties to the British government, but IRA involvement was never proven.

Whatever the cause of the fire, the Clotworthys and their Anglo-Irish friends got away unharmed, but an Irish servant girl named Ethel Gilligan was not so fortunate. She got trapped in an upper story. A local man heard her cries for help, scaled a ladder to the window where she stood pleading for help, and saved her. Sadly, she died shortly thereafter of smoke inhalation. Now she walks the grounds of the ruined castle at night in her white servant's frock. The locals call her the "White Lady."

The White Lady isn't alone in her nocturnal haunts. Every year on May 31, people swear they have seen an old coach drawn by four fine horses gallop down the road and disappear into the Long Pond, a prominent feature of the gardens. It is said that on the night of May 31, some time in the 18th century, a drunken coachman mistook the moonlit water as a road and drove his coach and all his passengers straight into the pond, where they all drowned.

County Antrim is home to numerous haunted castles. At Carrickfergus Castle, a soldier named Buttoncap haunts the walls and turrets in revenge for being executed for a crime he didn't commit. Two ghosts haunt Dunluce Castle—that of an English captain hanged by the clan MacDonnell, and a lovelorn girl named Maeve Roe who died in the tempestuous waters by the castle while trying to escape with her secret lover.

Carrickfergus Castle

When Shane's Castle caught fire in 1816, one of the dinner guests who fled the flames swore he saw a figure dressed in armor pass by an upstairs window.

Ballygally Castle in County Antrim is haunted by a most persistent spirit. This 17th century building was, like many other castles in Ireland, designed to be both a home and a fortress. With walls five feet thick, it could withstand light artillery, and its corner turrets allowed the guards to cover all approaches to the building. It was built by James Shaw, a Scottish immigrant, as an imitation of the baronial castles he was familiar with from his homeland. The Shaws lived in the castle for many generations, fighting off rebels during the rebellion of 1641 and again in 1689.

Kenneth Allen's picture of Ballygally Castle

It certainly looks like a good place for a ghost. The somber building stands on a hill overlooking the North Channel of the Irish Sea, and is lashed with wind and rain on many a dark night.

Residents have reported seeing a ghost since the 18th century, shortly after a certain Madame Nixon died there. She was a childless widow and sister-in-law of Henry Shaw, the squire of the period. She was a bit of a recluse and used to wander the castle halls for hours on end. When she died, she continued her aimless walks, clearly seen by numerous residents and visitors in her gray, silk dress. After a time her apparition faded, and now she is never seen, but the rustle of her silk dress is still heard by some who listen carefully.

Another resident spirit is Lady Isobel Shaw, who is usually spotted on the tower stairwell or walking along the halls, knocking on doors. She was the wife of James Shaw, the original builder. It is said she came to a tragic end when her firstborn turned out to be a daughter. James Shaw wanted a son to continue the family name and got so enraged that the child was a girl that he locked Lady Isobel in the drafty tower facing the sea and refused to feed her. Another version of the tale relates that James Shaw was angry because he discovered the child was the product of a dalliance Lady Isobel had with a strapping young fisherman. This would explain why Shaw didn't simply try again and wait to see the sex of the next child. Wherever the truth of the matter lies, into the tower Lady Shaw went. Starving and near death, she tried to climb out the window and down the wall, but she ultimately fell and died.

Today Ballygally Castle is a hotel, and even now, so long after Lady Shaw's death, guests are occasionally awoken by knocks on their door. When they answer, no one is there. Lady Shaw doesn't appear as much as she used to, but she still knocks.

It is interesting that there are so many tales of ghosts fading over time. They start out as both visual and auditory manifestations and slowly fade to faint sounds. The frequency of their hauntings also reduces with time. Some parapsychologists believe that the power that ties the spirit to this world runs out over time, like every other force in the universe. Some insist this is why people are not outnumbered by ghosts of cavemen, prehistoric Celts, and medieval peasants.

Irish folklore tells of certain places that are "thin," meaning they have only a thin barrier between this world and the next. While the entire world is like this at Halloween, in thin places it's like Halloween all year round. One of those thin places is Mahee Castle in County Down. Also known as Nendrum Castle, it is a forbidding ruin with a bloody history. It stands on a hill on Mahee Island near the western shore of Strangford Lough. Built in 1570 by Captain Thomas Browne, an English soldier sent to keep the peace, it changed hands several times in the many bitter wars between the English and the Irish. Archaeological evidence shows there may have been an earlier castle, or at least some sort of stone building, dating back to the Middle Ages.

So much bloodshed over so many years in a "thin" place is a recipe for haunting. Visitors to this lonely spot hear whispers as they walk through the ruin's halls, and many have reported strange mists appearing out of nowhere and coalescing into vague shapes. When this happens, no one sticks around to see what those shapes might become.

A different sort of spirit can be found at Crom Castle in County Fermanagh. This historic building is the seat of the Earl of Erne, at the center of a giant estate in the valley of the Upper Lough Erne. Actually it is two historic buildings, the "Old Castle" that dates to the seventeenth century, and the magnificent Victorian building erected in the nineteenth century, part of which is now a luxury hotel. Locals whisper that some of the Earls practiced black magic, and this is the cause of the peculiar apparition that sometimes plagues the noble family. A large round ball of white light will roll over the lake, warning the residents of the estate that something momentous will happen to the country. It appeared before national tragedies in the nineteenth century, and more recently in 1939 on the eve of World War Two, and again in 1971 to signal that the Troubles were about to enter one of their deadliest phases. Locals call this mysterious glow the "White Light of Crom."

Leap Castle in County Offaly is often called the world's most haunted castle, and while there is stiff competition for this dubious distinction, it is certainly a strong contender. This is one of the older castles in Ireland, built atop a Neolithic site and a building from the Iron Age dating to 500 BCE. The oldest part of the present structure is the main tower dating back to 1250. It served as the stronghold of the O'Bannon clan, the secondary chieftains of the region and under the rule of the more powerful O'Carroll clan.

D. Brands' picture of Leap Castle

By the 16th century the O'Carrolls had taken over the castle for themselves. They were a fractious bunch and spent much of their time with infighting and jockeying for power. In one particularly nasty incident in the 1530s, two brothers vied for dominance over the O'Carroll lands. One was a priest, and while he was performing Mass in the castle chapel in front of the family, his brother came in and stabbed him to death with a sword. The dead priest fell over the altar, smearing it with his blood. It is believed that the murderer flew into a rage because his priest brother started Mass without him, thus hinting that he wasn't important. Ever since, the place of this fratricide has been called the "Bloody Chapel." This wasn't the only murder within the family. Almost every generation was stained with some kinsman getting the blood of a relation on his hands.

During the English Civil War, the O'Carrolls supported King Charles, and thus when their side was defeated, they lost the castle and its land to the Darby family, stout supporters of Cromwell. The fighting in Ireland was especially bitter, with Cromwell slaughtering large numbers of Irish. The Royalist side was no less bloodthirsty, and when the Darbys took over the castle, it is said they took out three cartloads of skeletons from the dungeon, former guests of the O'Carrolls.

The castle's bloody history continued into modern times. During the Irish Civil War in 1922, local insurgents torched it. The new owners, the Dawkins family, had expanded the building and to pay for the costs had sold some of the land and raised rents for their remaining tenants. A group of armed men appeared in the middle of the night, forced the Dawkins family out, and burned down their home before their eyes while a crowd of locals gathered to watch and cheer.

The castle was gutted, but the strong walls remained intact. The castle is now under new management and is gradually being restored, and now that people are living there and visiting again, reports of ghostly sightings are on the rise. One of the centers for paranormal activity is the Bloody Chapel, scene of the notorious fratricide. Sometimes at night, neighbors will report that the chapel will light up, a brilliant illumination shining out of the arched windows. This phenomenon has been seen since the place was burned in 1922, and continues to be seen in the present day. Oddly, sometimes people visiting the place report smelling the stink of burnt rubber. No one has an explanation for this strange phenomenon. More understandable, and definitely more sinister, is the fact that the murdered O'Carroll priest is often seen walking silently through the chapel where he met his untimely death, or descending the nearby staircase on some mission known only to him.

The dungeon that the Darbys had to clean out is located just off of the Bloody Chapel, an odd place to put a prison but appropriate to the sensibilities of the O'Carrolls. The clan often poisoned henchmen and mercenaries who had outlived their usefulness and tossed their bodies into the dungeon. Those who didn't die from the poison died of starvation. Inevitably, the dungeon is haunted by the restless spirit of a former prisoner who can be seen leaving the dungeon, passing through the Bloody Chapel, and descending to the lower levels of the castle. Perhaps he's enjoying the freedom he lost in the last days of his life.

Not all the hauntings come from after the time of the fire. Many reports date to when the estate was active. During the time of the Darby residence, the house of the local priest stood not far from the main building. Those who slept there often complained about feeling a heavy weight on their bed in the middle of the night, or being awoken by snoring when they were alone in the room. On the back stairs near the servants' quarters people were sometimes startled to see a burly peasant pushing a large barrel up the back stairs. When he got to the top, the barrel would roll down and it and the peasant would disappear. There are also reports of a monk walking into the house through one window and out through another. The Priest's House, as it is locally known, is now a gutted ruin, but people still sometimes see shadowy figures flitting through the ruins.

Some of the most horrific tales of the hauntings of Leap Castle and the Priest's House come from an article written by Mildred Darby for a 1908 issue of the *Occult Review*. She collated numerous eyewitness accounts, both her own and those of her guests, and published them under a pseudonym in order to avoid scandal. An amateur occultist who performed séances in the castle, Mrs. Darby may have provoked the many spirits in the castle with her paranormal experiments. In the article she related several terrifying encounters with something she called "The Elemental." The following account happened to her personally:

"Suddenly, two hands were laid on my shoulders. I turned round sharply and saw, as clearly as I see you now—a grey 'Thing,' standing a couple of feet from me, with its bent arms raised as if it were cursing me. I cannot describe in words how utterly awful the 'Thing' was, its very undefinableness rendering the horrible shadow more gruesome. Human in shape, a little shorter than I am, I could just make out the shape of big black holes like great eyes and sharp features, but the whole figure-head, face, hands and all-was grey-unclean, bluish grey, something of the colour and appearance of common cotton wool. But, oh! so sinister, repulsive and devilish. My friends who are clever about occult things say it is what they call an 'Elemental.'

"The thing was about the size of a sheep, thin, gaunt and shadowy in parts. Its face was human, or to be more accurate, inhuman, in its vileness, with large holes of blackness for eyes, loose slobbery lips, and a thick saliva-dripping jaw, sloping back suddenly into its neck! Nose it had none, only spreading, cancerous cavities, the whole face being a uniform tint of grey. This too, was the colour of the dark coarse hair covering its head, neck and body. Its forearms were thickly coated with the same hair, so were its paws, large, loose and hand-shaped; and it sat on its hind legs, one hand or paw was raised, and a claw-like finger was extended ready to scratch the paint. Its lustreless eyes, which seemed half decomposed, and looked incredibly foul, stared into mine, and the horrible smell which had before offended my nostrils, only a hundred times intensified, came up to my face, filling me with a deadly nausea. I noticed the lower half of the creature was indefinite and seemed semi-transparent at least, I could see the framework of the door that led into the gallery through its body."

A friend of Mildred Darby's wrote her a letter about an experience with the Elemental they had together. "I saw your eyes fixed upon something above our heads, and the next minute my own eyes were filled by the sight of a Thing in the gallery looking down at us. There was plenty of light from the lamps in the hall and the one above on the wall at the corner of the gallery, for every one of us to see quite plainly the grey-coloured figure about the height of a small grown-up person looking down at us. I wish I thought I could ever forget the sight of that grey figure with dark spots like holes in its head instead of eyes, standing with grey arms folded on the gallery railing looking down at us…Then just as he put foot on the gallery, the Thing that he saw there, that we were watching, suddenly faded out of sight. The Thing did not move, only became less and less visible until it vanished."

Mrs. Darby's final encounter with the entity is recorded later in the article. "On the 25th Nov 1915 two of our servants knowing the master would be late and that I was driving that afternoon had invited friends, two soldiers from the Barracks at Birr distant the other side 6 miles. They came rather late and my husband came home early so the visitors had to be kept out of his sight in the lower regions of one of the wings (the Priests House) and were unable to be shown the centre tower – the very lofty hall. At 7:15 my husband and I went up to dress for dinner, my room in extremity of house from kitchens, his dressing room next door to me. Whilst dressing I was startled by a loud yell of terror stricken male and female voices coming apparently from the hall—and ran out to see the cause. My husband was out ahead of me at his heels I passed through corridor of wing and onto the gallery wing rounds two sides of hall. [There were] two lamps on gallery, two more in hall below. On the gallery leaning with 'hands' resting on its rail I saw the Thing—the Elemental and smelt it only too well. At the same moment my husband pulled up sharply about 10 feet from the Thing, and half turning let fly a volley of abuse at me ending up 'Dressing up a thing like that to try and make a fool of me. And now you'll say I've seen something and I have not seen anything and there is nothing to see, or ever was.' This last speech [he said] without a pause, and began waving one hand at the Thing ending up by stalking back to his dressing room still abusing me for trying to give him a fright. As he was speaking the Elemental grew fainter and fainter in its outlines until it disappeared. By the sounds from my husband's room I judged he was employed as I was myself in preparing an empty spot for our coming dinner. He never made any enquiry as to the yell that called us both out, and from that day to this has not mentioned the incident to me. I heard from our servants that when we went to dress for dinner they had brought their friends just to show them the hall, when all four has suddenly seen and smelt the Elemental looking down at them from the gallery. We all got such a turn, we couldn't help letting out a bawl then fled to servants quarters where all four were very sick."

The two maids who had seen the Elemental quit the next day.

While some may think, as Mr. Darby did, that the Elemental had been made up by Mildred Darby as a way of getting attention, sightings continue to this day, long after Mildred's death. Witnesses all give the same general description of the creature.

Just what the Elemental is remains a matter of debate among historians and parapsychologists. One theory is that it is a guardian summoned to the spot by druids to protect their sacred site. Others hold that it was intended as a sort of weapon used by the Earl of Kildare, Gerald Fitzgerald. A leading occultist, he was a rival of the O'Carroll clan and might have summoned the Elemental to destroy the castle from within. That it has failed for several centuries just goes to show that you can't get good help from the other side. Another story, favored by many in the local area, is that the Elemental is the ghost of one of the O'Carroll family who died of leprosy, hence the horrid features.

Another spirit that may be the result of O'Carroll cruelty is the Red Lady. This is an apparition of a young woman clad in red that shines with an eerie glow. She carries a knife in her hand and when she appears, the room becomes unbearably cold. She is said to be the victim of an assault by one of the O'Carroll clan. Kept captive for his pleasure, the woman eventually gave birth. The cruel man then killed his own child, not wanting to take care of it. When this happened, the Red Lady grabbed the knife and plunged it in her own breast. A visitor to the castle related her experience with the Red Lady to the *Occult Review*. "On the 31st of October I went to my bedroom about 11pm. During the night, the time was 12.45am, as I subsequently saw by my watch, I felt that I was awakened by somebody in my room. It was pitch dark and at first I could see nothing. I was wide awake with an extraordinary cold feeling at my heart that rapidly increased in intensity. Almost immediately I felt, as much as saw, that there was a tall figure in the middle of the room. My first impression was that O'Connoll [sic] himself was there, as no other member of the household would correspond to the height. 'What is it?' I asked. There was no answer, but now I could see, dimly at first and with increasing distinctness, that the tall figure was clothed from head to foot in red, and with its right hand raised menacingly in the air. To my utter astonishment I could see that the light which illuminated the figure was from within, having very much the effect of the dark lantern used in a photographer's room. As the figure advanced towards me the light increased, and I could see distinctly that the form was that of a very tall woman holding some sort of a weapon, knife or dagger in her hand. 'What is it?' I asked again, adding 'Who is it?' and then hurriedly struck a match and lit my candle. As the flame of the match and candle illuminated the room I looked all around. The room was empty."

. One of these haunted buildings is Ross Castle, on the shores of Lough Sheelin, County Meath, which has earned the dubious distinction of being considered the most haunted castle in Ireland. The region had a bloody history in the Middle Ages, having been just "beyond the pale," meaning it was past the area of English control. With the English to the east and the native Celtic tribes to the west and north, the area became a constant battleground. Several castles and strongholds dotted the landscape at the time. Ross Castle was built in 1533 by the English to control the River Inny where it enters Lough Sheelin. This was the outer limits of their territory, and thus the castle was of crucial strategic importance. It suffered many sieges and battles before it was eventually leveled by Oliver Cromwell after it had been used as a base for Irish rebels.

A 19th century picture of Ross Castle

A modern picture of Ross Castle

Cromwell

Naturally, such a place was ripe for haunting. Most of the stories center around Richard Nugent, the 12th Lord of Delvin, the man who built the castle in 1536. He was a tough and cruel man, even by the standards of those tough and cruel times, and it eventually earned him the nickname of the Black Baron. Some locals say this was due to his having hanged an innocent beggar whom he accused of stealing some bread, even though there had been no evidence against the man.

Blood does not always run true, and the Black Baron's daughter was said to be as kind as he was cruel; as sweet as he was bitter. Her name was Sabina, and everyone loved her. She could often be seen strolling on the shores of the Lough Sheelin, where she would admire the view and speak with anyone she met without prejudice. Even though she was the daughter of an English military occupier, she chatted happily with the Irish peasants she met. This made her as well loved by the Irish as she was by the English.

Given her position, she was supposed to be accompanied by a chaperone at all times. Sabina had a free spirit, however, and often slipped away to walk alone, knowing she had nothing to fear.

It was on one of those solitary walks that she met a handsome young man and started talking with him. His name was Orwin O'Reilly, the son of a local Irish chief. They formed an instant attraction for one another and promised to meet again, soon. Neither Sabina nor Orwin were so young and innocent as to be unaware of the dangers of their friendship. Their fathers were enemies, after all, as were their respective peoples, and they had to have their meetings in the utmost of secrecy. As the meetings continued, their love grew, as did their despair. They wanted to get married, but this was impossible; simply meeting together as they did was bound to cause a war.

Like other star-crossed lovers throughout time, they decided to elope. One night, Sabina slipped out of Ross Castle and crept to the shore of Lough Sheelin, where Orwin waited for her with a boat. They rowed out across the water, their young hearts filled with hope for the future that they would settle down somewhere far away from their warring fathers and start a new life under new names.

As the lovers talked of the future, a sudden storm blew in from the west. Orwin tried to manage the oars while Sabina bailed desperately, but it was no use. The storm grew stronger, eventually overturning the boat and sending the couple into the frigid waters of Lough Sheelin. Sabina was found the next morning, washed up on shore and barely alive. She was carried back to Ross Castle where she lay unconscious for three days. When she, at last, awoke, it was to terrible news - her lover, Orwin, had been found as well, but he had drowned. Sabina fell into despair and locked herself in the tower, refusing to eat or drink until she, too, had died. Perhaps she hoped to join her lover on the other side, but it was not to be. Instead, she haunts the castle, endlessly roaming its halls or looking over its battlements with the hope of finding her long-lost lover, her sorrowful wailing awakening residents.

A picture of Lough Sheelin

The Black Baron is sometimes seen, too. According to local legend, Sabina's stay on this earth will only end when her evil father has atoned for his misdeeds.

Ross Castle is now a bed and breakfast, and online guest reviews tell of the many strange occurrences happening there. Besides seeing both ghosts, one visitor was scratched on the arm by invisible nails, cutting so deeply they drew blood. Others hear strains of old music, feel sudden drops in temperature, and are awoken by phantom footsteps in the hall. The hauntings center around the tower, the oldest part of the castle, although entities have been seen, heard, and felt all over the newer portions built in the last two centuries, as well. Of all the rooms in the bed and breakfast, the most haunted is the Whisper Room, so called because guests there often hear whispering that seems to come from thin air.

Even for those who don't believe in ghosts, a stay in an old castle is a memorable experience. Ross Castle is decorated with suits of armor, stuffed birds, and even a buffalo's head, which–while not exactly Irish–certainly adds an odd atmosphere to the place. Several other Irish castles have been turned into similar B&Bs as well, such as Clontarf Castle in Dublin, Ashford Castle in County Mayo, Ballynahinch Castle in County Connemara, and many more. All of them, it seems, have a ghost story to tell.

Ireland's Other Haunted Historic Buildings

Castles aren't the only places where the spirits of the dead linger. Many of Ireland's other historic buildings are home to a ghost or two.

Several can be found in and around Dublin. By far the most notorious are the ruins of the Hellfire Club visible atop Mount Pelier, one the Dublin Mountains a little way outside of town. This grim stone building, which looks a bit like a medieval church, was built in 1725 by William Conolly, a local rake and speaker of the Irish parliament in Dublin, as a meeting place for his debauched friends. To save money he reused the stones of a prehistoric passage grave he found on the site. These underground tombs were made in the shape of subterranean stone hallways and contained the bones of numerous individuals put there over a period of time. What Conolly did with the bones is not recorded. As a final touch, he removed a menhir, or Neolithic sacred standing stone, and used it as a lintel over the fireplace. It appealed to his dark sense of humor to use such pagan remains as part of his pleasure retreat. Perhaps he hoped to summon some spirits that way too.

Hellfire Clubs were all the rage in the eighteenth century. The first was founded in London in 1718, by Philip, Duke of Wharton. The most famous Hellfire Club was the one founded in England by Sir Francis Dashwood. It met from around 1749 to around 1760 and created several scandals thanks to its wild parties and strange rituals that mocked the church.

Conolly's Dublin Hellfire Club proved no better. It was billed as a hunting lodge for gentlemen, but soon rumors began to fly of strange goings-on within its walls.

It is hard to separate fact from fiction when it comes to Hellfire Clubs. How much were they simply the drinking dens of the rich and dissolute, and how much were they meeting grounds for sinister rituals? No doubt this varied from club to club, but the spirits that linger in the clubhouse in the Dublin mountains show that Conolly and his friends were up to more than just drinking and fornicating. Plus there is good evidence that their favorite drink was "scaltheen," a mixture of whiskey and hot butter, which showed poor taste if not diabolical inspiration.

It is said the members of the Hellfire Club worshipped the Devil in a blasphemous imitation of Church ritual, and that when they sat down to dine, they left a place for the Dark Lord in case he wanted to join them. Apparently he did show up one night when the gentlemen were playing cards. He asked to join them and the members, thinking he was simply another upper class Irishman passing through, offered him the Devil's seat as a joke. Soon they were all drinking and betting and having a great time. Later in the evening, one of the players dropped a card, and when he reached down to pick it up, noticed the newcomer had cloven hooves instead of feet. When the startled man pointed this out, the stranger turned into a ball of fire and shot away.

To placate their evil master, the dissolute rakes would sacrifice animals and maybe even human beings. Other acts of cruelty abounded, such as lighting cats on fire and laughing hysterically as they watched the poor creatures run in terror and pain down the hill. A local farmer boasted that he wasn't afraid of these degenerate gentlemen and went up the hill one night to find out if the rumors were true. He was found the next day wandering aimlessly, having been struck deaf and mute. The poor man never regained his faculties. It was like his mind had been wiped clean of whatever he had seen in the clubhouse on the hill.

The members of the Hellfire Club were certainly not averse to murder. One of their victims was a young dwarf. What he did to anger the young aristocrats is unclear. Perhaps they were just bored and felt like killing someone. Now his spirit can be seen haunting the ruins of the club as well as a nearby house called Killakee House. This building was used as the clubhouse for a time after the main clubhouse was damaged by fire and had to undergo repairs. The fire was said to have been caused when a footman accidentally spilled a drink on a Hellfire Club member's coat. The "gentleman" was so enraged he poured brandy over the hapless servant and set him on fire. The fire spread to consume the building.

A strange confirmation about these terrible goings-on came in 1971 when a shallow grave was uncovered under the kitchen of Killakee House. It contained the skeleton of a dwarf.

Those who venture into the ruins of the clubhouse these days have reported several different supernatural manifestations. People who enter this unholy place with crosses around their necks are liable to have them yanked off by unseen hands. Others catch a whiff of brimstone while walking through the ruins, perhaps because this has become a "thin" place, where the barrier between this world and the next have been eroded by the numerous black masses and sacrifices done on this spot.

The Killakee House has its own spirits. Some of them manifest only as the sounds of ringing bells, while others appear as faint images. These include three people who supposedly took part in black masses at the house—an Indian gentleman and two nuns called Holy Mary and Blessed Margaret.

The area is also the haunt of an elemental spirit called the Black Cat of Killakee. This supernatural creature takes the form of a huge, black cat the size of a Dalmatian with a humanlike but twisted face. While it is tempting to think of it as a vengeful spirit angered by the torture of so many cats on the site, occultists say it is in fact an elemental spirit that only superficially looks like a feline. It can speak in a human voice but if you bump into it at night, the best response is not to start a conversation but to run away screaming. That will most likely come naturally.

Others have heard the screaming cries for help of an agonized young woman, said to be the spirit of a girl who was stuffed in a barrel, the barrel set alight, and then rolled down the hill. The good members of the Hellfire Club had tired of cats, apparently.

The malevolent atmosphere created by Conolly and his friends lingers on every part of Mount Pelier. The housing estates at the foot of the mountain report persistent paranormal events ranging from strange smells and poltergeist activity to spiritual apparitions.

While the members of the Hellfire Club tried to become friends with the master of hell, some people created Hell right here on Earth. One of these is Kilmainham Gaol, a harsh prison called by some of its inmates "the darkest hole in all of Ireland."

The government built Kilmainham Gaol in 1796 on Gallows Hill as a county prison, holding men, women, and children all in the same wing and sometimes even in the same cell. Countless prisoners fell victim to further crimes at the hands of the stronger and more aggressive inmates. The jail was also the final destination of several Irish revolutionaries. In its first year of operation Henry Joy McCracken, one of the founders of the United Irishmen, was jailed here until his hanging two years later. After the 1916 Easter Uprising, many leading revolutionaries such as Pádraig Pearse and James Connolly were incarcerated here. Fourteen of them were executed in the yard. During the Great Potato Famine, the jail became packed with starving people whose only crime was begging or stealing food.

Kilmainham Gaol became known as a place of executions, torture, and neglect. In earlier years prisoners would be hanged right outside the front gate. It is no wonder that unhappy spirits linger there. The prison closed in 1924 and was left to deteriorate. By 1960 it was falling apart, but the determined efforts of the Kilmainham Jail Restoration Society have since turned it into one of Dublin's star tourist attractions.

A picture of the jail's main hall

During the restoration, the workmen discovered that the jail was not entirely empty. A painter working in the basement found himself picked up by a strong wind that blew out of nowhere and pressed him against a wall, holding him there for several seconds. The man fled, never to return. Others heard voices and the sound of slamming doors in wings of the prison where no one was known to be. Most of the voices sounded like children begging to be set free. The tramp of booted feet from spectral guards was a common occurrence. The director of the restoration, Dan McGill, lived in the prison while it was being restored in order to devote his entire time to it and also act as a watchman. One night he noticed the lights to the prison chapel were on. He went and switched them off, only for them to turn back on again. This happened several times during the night, keeping Mr. McGill from getting any sleep.

Even after being open to the public for years, the spirits remain at Kilmainham Gaol. Visitors report feelings of being watched, or hearing the guards and child prisoners. Some children (living ones) have refused to enter the prison despite the encouragement of their parents. Parapsychologists say that children are more sensitive to the spirit world because they have had less societal conditioning and thus their minds are more open. Because of this, some children sense the malevolent or anguished spirits within and beg their parents not to make them go on the tour.

Many of Ireland's traditional pubs are believed to be haunted as well. John Kavanagh's in Dublin, locally known as "The Gravediggers Pub," dates back to 1833, making it a relative youngster when compared to the city's historic buildings. It gets its nickname thanks to being located next to the historic Glasnevin Cemetery, where many prominent Irish figures, such as Irish nationalists Stewart Parnell and Roger Casement, are buried. The pub was where the gravediggers were known to refresh themselves after a hard day's work, often making their orders by throwing a clod of dirt against the wall in order to alert the barkeep. At night, it was said to be the den of grave robbers. It is still a solemn place, with no singing or dancing allowed, and no television that ruins the atmosphere of so many old pubs. There isn't even a telephone.

Parnell

Casement

On some quiet nights, a visitor might notice an old man in an out of date tweed suit, sipping a pint at the end of the bar. He doesn't speak, and is so unremarkable that no one bothers to speak to him, but when he finishes his drink he simply fades away.

Haunted Irish Graveyards

Ghosts naturally linger around the places where they were interred, and Ireland's historic graveyards are supposedly full of them.

One of the more frightening examples is Kilbride Graveyard in Arklow, County Wicklow. Within its grounds stands the unusual mausoleum of the Wicklow family. Built by Ralph Howard, the 1st Viscount Wicklow, in the 1780s in the shape of a 30 foot high pyramid with an entrance in the style of an Egyptian temple, it was said to have been inspired by the symbolism of Freemasonry. The mortal remains of a total of eighteen members of the Wicklow family rest inside but the mausoleum contains darker secrets. Local rumors recount that one night a child's pitiful cries were heard coming from within. Once the local people got over their fear of ghosts, they opened up the mausoleum and found a toddler inside, wailing next to the rotting coffins of the Wicklow family. The child was very much alive but too young and too frightened to tell how he had been entombed in the Wicklow mausoleum. After that, the tomb was permanently sealed and the Wicklows told to bury their dead elsewhere.

Memories of an even greater tragedy still haunt the Old Church Cemetery in Cobh, County Cork. It was there that more than 200 bodies from the *RMS Lusitania* were interred in a mass grave. The *Lusitania* was a British ocean liner sailing from New York City to Liverpool when on May 7, 1915, it was torpedoed by a German U-boat. The ship, its passengers, and crew were only the latest of countless victims of Germany's "unrestricted submarine warfare" policy, an attempt to stop all shipping to the island kingdom in order to break the British economy and force it to drop out of World War I. More than 1,100 passengers and crew died, including more than 120 Americans. This helped turn American opinion in favor of intervention in the European war, although it would take the United States government another two years to actually declare war on Germany.

The monument to those who died in the sinking is well-maintained and frequently visited by historians and school groups, but it appears to be visited by other entities as well. Sometimes at night people have heard the solemn music and lowered voices of the original funeral procession that laid the victims in their final resting place.

Shankill Graveyard in Lurgan, County Armagh, had the distinction of once being haunted by someone who wasn't even dead. In 1705, local woman Marjorie McCall contracted a bad fever and appeared to die. Her husband was a physician and examined her body. He could find no sign of breathing or a heartbeat. Others checked on her too and concurred with the grieving widower. She was given last rites and buried, but her rest was disturbed that same night by a group of resurrection men. This special form of grave robber dated to a time when dissection was illegal. Surgeons could only get bodies to examine when some foul criminal was executed and, as an added punishment for their crimes, was handed over to the surgeons. The fear of dissection stems from the belief that one's body must remain whole for the Second Coming of Christ when all the dead will rise from their graves. So resurrection men were paid good money to supply bodies of the newly dead to surgeons, who could then gain knowledge of human anatomy.

When the resurrection men opened Marjorie McCall's coffin, they found her body well preserved, as it had only been interred a few hours before. They must have smiled as they hauled her out and put her in the back of their cart, because fresh bodies commanded the highest price. No self-respecting physician wanted to practice their dissection skills on a stinking, moldering corpse. Then the resurrection men spied a gold wedding ring on her finger. Not only had they gotten themselves a fresh one, but she apparently came with a bonus. The grave robbers tried to remove it but found her fingers had swollen, perhaps due to the fever she had suffered before she died. One of the grave robbers pulled out a knife and started sawing through poor Marjorie's finger. Just then she sat bolt upright in the back of the cart. She had most likely been in a coma and the pain of the blade cutting through her flesh woke her out of it. The grave robbers fled in mortal terror as she leapt out of the cart and ran into the night.

Marjorie staggered home, pounding on the door to be let in. Her husband John had been sitting inside with their children, grieving, when they heard the knock. John McCall commented that if he hadn't known better, he would have sworn that it sounded like his wife's knock. He went to the door and was so stunned to see his dead wife standing there dripping blood that he dropped dead himself. He was buried in the grave that she had been taken out of.

Marjorie McCall eventually did die a few years later and her gravestone bears the inscription, "Died once, buried twice." It can still be seen today.

Haunted Houses

It is not just castles that become the home to restless spirits. Humbler homes can be haunted as well. The worst case in the whole country was a little three-room cottage near Cooneen, County Fermanagh. At the beginning of the twentieth century, the Murphy family lived there, including Michael and Bridget, plus a son and six daughters. They all lived quite peacefully until Michael died in a freak accident in 1907. Not long after, strange things began to happen.

At first it was the front door. At all times of the day or night the Murphy family would hear someone knocking on it. When they'd answer, no one was there. Then the knocking began to spread, as if someone was pounding on the windows or walls or even the roof. This was followed by heavy footsteps in the attic, which the family used as a hayloft. No one was ever caught making these sounds and the Murphy family became convinced that they were not victims of some cruel practical joker, but rather a poltergeist.

A poltergeist is a particular type of entity that is never seen, instead manifesting itself with noises and moving objects. The name comes from German and literally means "noisy ghost." The ghost at the Murphy cottage certainly became noisy.

Soon it was getting violent as well, tossing plates across the room to smash them against the walls, or lifting up beds into the air and dropping them back onto the floor. Neighbors witnessed these things too, and the Murphy cottage became the talk of the county.

Desperate, Bridget Murphy brought in Father Eugene Coyle and Father Peter Smythe from Maguiresbridge. The startled priests saw objects fly across the room and strange shapes appear on the walls, morphing as if they had a life of their own. Snores and hissing sounds came from the shadows. Father Smythe was sitting on a bed while this was happening and felt something squirming under the sheets. He told the spirit to leave and felt a rat under his hand, and then an invisible serpent wrap around his wrist.

The two priests went away shaking with fear. The poltergeist activity became so well known that it even brought the attention of the journalist Cahir Healy, who later became a minister of parliament. He visited the cottage to write about it and saw the manifestations for himself.

At times the poltergeist showed a less malevolent side. If anyone played music in the house, a popular pastime in the days before television and radio, the poltergeist would thump on the walls in time with the tune. At times the unseen entity would give them a tune of its own, usually an old one like "The Soldier's Song."

Father Coyle returned to the cottage with permission from his superiors to perform an exorcism. This only seemed to anger the poltergeist. As he was intoning the sacred formula to rid the house of spirits, groans emanated from the hayloft, sheets rose up from the beds in menacing shapes, and objects flew across the room. The spirit did not leave. A second exorcism also failed.

To make matters worse for the Murphys, the neighbors began to blame them for the poltergeist. They claimed the son, James, was practicing black magic. They said he had found a book in the forest called *The Legions of Doom* that told him how to raise devils from Hell and that this was what had led to the hauntings. The Murphys found themselves rejected by the community.

By 1913 they had had enough and left Ireland for the United States. Unfortunately, the poltergeist followed them, making noises in their cabin as they crossed the Atlantic. So many passengers complained about the noise that the captain himself came down to their cabin and told them to behave. He did not believe them when they said that they were victims of a poltergeist who had moved house. In America the trouble persisted and one of the daughters ended up in a lunatic asylum, her sanity shredded by what she had experienced. Eventually, though, the poltergeist became less and less active until it vanished altogether.

No one ever knew if the spirit was that of Michael, who died just before the trouble started, or came from some other cause. Paranormal investigators point out that poltergeists often occur in homes with adolescent girls and may in fact be caused by them. The Murphy home had three girls going through puberty during those years and some investigators believe their anxiety at the loss of their father had led them to subconsciously create the hauntings. Indeed, the two priests noted that the manifestations seemed to center around Annie, the eldest daughter.

The cottage still stands today although it is deep in the woods and in a sad state of disintegration. Now it's a hangout for local teenagers attracted by its grim reputation, and the fact that adults steer clear of the place.

A few years ago, the County Antrim Paranormal Research Association visited the cottage at night, setting up audio and night vision equipment as well as a detector for electromagnetic pulses. One of the investigators played "The Soldier's Song" on a penny whistle and noted several spikes on the pulse detector. The audio equipment also picked up several sounds of movement in the house when the team wasn't there although the cameras saw nothing. Later, they heard the faint sound of a penny whistle coming from the surrounding woods.

The little village of Delvin, County Westmeath, has a disproportionate number of ghostly residents. The local castle, Ballinlough Castle, of course has several. Strange lights, a phantom carriage, and a spectral girl seem to be required of Irish castles.

The parish meeting place, St. Patrick's Hall, serves as an events venue and remains a popular spot for the villagers to get together. Built in 1832 as a chapel, modern visitors are sometimes reminded of its original use by the spectral presence of a priest. Nowadays he is only felt or heard, not seen. He seems to linger around the stage area where he once gave his sermons. People report an unsettling feeling there, and caretakers locking up late at night have heard footsteps, seen odd lights with no known origins, and heard the piano playing all by itself.

In earlier times the priest was more active. It was said that when the living priest heard confessions late at night, the last person to give confession had to walk him home, or the spirit of his predecessor would walk with the priest instead!

Another church, St. Mary's, dates back to the fourteenth century and has been abandoned since the 1970s. It is now derelict and in a poor state of repair. Sometimes vague shapes can be seen peeking out of the shutters of its crumbling tower. The grounds are also said to be home to a banshee.

Another local tale tells how the well-to-do Howard Fetherstonhaugh of nearby Bracklyn was murdered in 1868. His wife learned of his death when she heard a knock on the door, opened it, and was faced with his bloody ghost.

The village even has a haunted golf course. The Delvin Golf Club is located on Cottages Hill, where once two sisters lived in a modest cottage. It is said that one murdered the other and now the victim's spirit wanders the golf course and surrounding woods at night. She's known as the "White Lady."

The most haunted building in Delvin was the Castle Inn, home to the spirit of a blacksmith who was perhaps the original landlord. When he died early in the past century, he could be seen standing at the door to his pub, watching his own funeral procession pass by.

In the late 20th century, the children of the new landlord repeatedly saw a frightening man in the bar area when the pub was closed, and refused to watch television in the room. The landlord himself felt an eerie presence on numerous occasions.

Out of respect for this local specter, when the pub was abandoned and boarded up, someone painted the blacksmith on the front door. Perhaps this was a sort of apology for his legacy being condemned to demolition. If it was, the apology was not accepted. As the demolition crew was wrecking the building with bulldozers, they accidentally knocked down a power cable, electrocuting the whole street. Luckily no one was hurt, but one workman was stuck in the cab of his digger until the power could be cut off. As he sat there, he noticed a man, dressed in the clothes of a former century, walking through the rubble, completely unaffected by the surging charge of electricity.

The pub was demolished in 2005 to make way for a youth center and a credit union. As of this date, the kids and bankers haven't noticed any ghosts.

The Renvyle House Hotel in Connemara, County Galway, is rife with ghosts. A boy of only 14 is said to have strangled himself to death with his bare hands in the building. How this is possible is a bit of a mystery, but his restless spirit lingers to this day.

The house, which offers stunning views from a cliff overlooking Galway Bay and out into the North Atlantic, was first converted into a hotel in 1883 by the Blake family. Owing to its luxury accommodation and pleasant surroundings, it attracted esteemed guests such as Winston Churchill and W.B. Yeats. It is unclear when the hauntings started. The first person to record them was Dr. Oliver St. John Gogarty, who in addition to being a physician and poet, decided to become a hotel owner as well and bought the property in 1917.

Shortly after becoming the new owner, he was sitting in his room when he heard loud footsteps thumping down the hallway outside his door. Lighting a candle, he went out to investigate. As soon as he went into the hall, a cold wind blew out the light and he suddenly felt weak, as if all his limbs were tied down.

The servants had similar experiences, and refused to sleep in one of the upstairs rooms reserved for their use. It was an odd room, with barred windows set high on the uppermost floor. Anyone who slept there felt menacing presences and insisted on moving their quarters elsewhere. One night they heard something heavy scrape across the floor in that room and bang against the inside of the door. Plucking up their courage, they tried to open it but discovered a heavy weight on the inside. No amount of pushing could budge the door. The next day they propped a ladder up to the window and peeked in. A large storage chest had been pushed against the door to block it. No one was in the room and the windows were barred. The servants had to pry the bars loose to get into the door and move the chest back into place.

Dr. Gogarty, being a poet as well as the victim of various ghosts, often had Ireland's literary set staying at his hotel. One regular guest was Yeats. His wife Georgia Yeats was interested in spiritualism, as many respectable people were in those days. It was quite common for the middle and upper classes to hold séances in their home or invite leading spiritualists over to address gatherings of their friends.

Ghosts and poltergeists often increase their activities when someone who is spiritually sensitive comes near, and this was the case when Georgia stayed at the hotel. Doors would open and shut, cold winds blew from nowhere, and strange noises were heard. Georgia, Yeats, and Dr. Gogarty decided to hold a séance to find out the origins of the disturbances.

Georgia made contact with a spirit, whose disembodied voice told her that it didn't want people living in the house. The hauntings were its attempts to get them to leave. This is a common occurrence, where ghosts are stuck between the world of the living and the world of the dead and wish only to be left in peace. What they really need, occultists say, is to accept their fate and move on to the afterlife where they can finally rest. The ghost said that if Georgia would enter a certain room alone, it would appear to her.

Just why Yeats would let his wife enter a room alone with a ghost, or why his wife would do such a thing, is unclear, but go she did, and what she saw has forever become part of the lore of the Renvyle House Hotel. She entered the room and immediately saw a thin vapor hovering near the fireplace. It coalesced into the form of a fourteen year old boy with red hair and pale skin. His face was stamped with an expression of immeasurable suffering.

After the visitation, Georgia Yeats researched the house and found that the boy had, indeed, existed. He had been part of the Blake family and had killed himself for some unknown reason.

Another visitor to the hotel, Evan Morgan, tried to exorcise the ghost but failed in a most spectacular way. He went into the haunted room and began the holy rite to cast out evil spirits. Instead, it was he who was cast out. The vapor reappeared and Morgan felt a great force throw him down on the floor. Then the vapor formed into the pale, redheaded boy. This time the boy grasped his own neck with his hands as if to strangle himself. Morgan lay helpless on the floor, crying out with terror until his friends rushed in and pulled him to safety. By then the boy had vanished, but his legend lives on.

A few years after Gogarty bought the property, the IRA burnt the house down. This wasn't done because they had anything against ghosts, but because they didn't like rich landowners. Many historic buildings suffered the same fate in the 1920s. Gogarty rebuilt it in 1930, and discovered to his dismay that the ghosts had moved into the new building. Apparently ghosts don't let terrorists dictate their hauntings.

Nowadays guests complain of odd noises, apparitions gliding down the hallways, and sheets being pulled off them by invisible hands in the middle of the night. The most frequent sighting happens when female guests are looking into the mirror while putting on their make-up. They are startled to see the reflection of a man behind them. When they turn around, no one is there.

Other Haunted Places

Ghosts are not always content to lurk indoors, but sometimes venture out into the Irish countryside. They have a special affinity for what folklorists call "liminal places," those that are on the borders of one place and another such as crossroads and bridges. These places are especially susceptible to magical influence.

Blackwater Bridge between Sneem and Kenmare, in County Kerry, is one such place. In a tale collected in the 1890s by ethnographer Jeremiah Curtin, the local people recounted a strange occurrence related to this bridge.

The bridge had often been the scene for a frightening apparition of a headless horseman. These figures are found all over Ireland, England, and Scotland and are one of the staples of ghost lore. The local people near Blackwater Bridge believed in the legend well enough, however, and stayed away from the bridge at night.

One evening a man named Martin Doyle, who worked on an estate outside Sneem, needed to have a letter delivered to town. Not having the time to do it himself, he looked around for someone to walk into Sneem for him. As it had already turned dark, no one wanted to go for fear of spirits abroad at night. Finally his cousin James volunteered, declaring that he was afraid of nothing, living or dead. Martin thanked his cousin and gave him the letter as well as a steel sword to protect himself.

A good length of steel is essential for anyone who might come into contact with hostile ghosts. Steel has magical properties against the spirit world, much like silver does against lycanthropes, and steel made by an Irish blacksmith is twice as efficacious.

So James set out for Sneem with the trusty sword at his belt. Being the brave sort, he didn't even stick to the main road but took shortcuts on lonely paths through wildlands and woods. He had made it about halfway to Sneem when a ghost appeared in his path, blocking his way. The ghost rushed at him, but James drew his sword and swiped at the spirit. The ghost backed off, and James hurried on his way, but the ghost dogged him for some time, occasionally rushing at James but darting back every time the man swung his steel blade. At last they came to a crossroads near Sneem and the ghost disappeared.

Relieved, James hurried on into town. He may have been brave, but even he wanted this trip to be over. Once he got to his destination, however, he discovered that the gentleman to whom he was to deliver the letter had moved six miles away to a spot just on the opposite side of Blackwater Bridge.

The bridge already had a bad reputation, but a promise is a promise and James was good to his word. He walked the six miles to the bridge without incident, and just as he crossed the bridge another ghost attacked him. This one was especially vicious, much more dangerous than the fist one. It couldn't stand to face steel, however, and James fought him off as he made his way across the bridge, hoping he'd get to the gentleman's house before the ghost slipped through his guard.

James had almost made it across the bridge when he saw a headless horseman galloping along the riverbank on the opposite side. The rider drove his horse straight up a nearby cliff. When the ghost saw the headless horseman, it immediately went after it and both disappeared in the night.

James got to his destination just as the cock crowed. The gentleman was surprised to hear how far James had walked, and told him that the ghost chased the headless horseman every night, although no one knew why. James received a handsome tip for his trouble and the reputation as a fearless man. His name has been remembered in tales in the local area for more than a century now.

Then there is the strange tale of the *Nellie Flemming*, a three-masted schooner lost at sea with all hands. Before this happened, a group of fishermen sailed out into Whiting Bay near Ardmore, County Waterford, one Sunday night in February of 1936. They were fishing in secret. Not only were they committing the sin of working on a Sunday, but they were not allowed to fish in those waters. Their plan was to lay the nets and come back the next night to collect them.

The fishermen started putting out the nets when they saw a weak light out to sea. Worried that it might be a patrol boat full of customs officials, who often sailed the area at night looking for people smuggling or fishing illegally, they hurriedly pulled in their nets and sailed away around the head of the bay. But as they moved off, they clearly saw a three-masted schooner sailing into the bay. Although the ship was illuminated with a soft glow like a candle, no one was visible on deck. It made no sound and made not even a ripple as it passed through the water.

Some of the fishermen felt sure they'd seen a phantom ship, a portent of a maritime disaster. Many such ghost ships had been seen in the bay and indeed all around Ireland. Even those among the crew who dismissed the idea of a ghost ship were sufficiently rattled that they decided to do their fishing on another night.

Then, only two weeks later, the *Nellie Flemming* was making her way to Youghal, County Cork, a little way along the coast from Ardmore Bay, when she was caught in a storm and sank with all hands. After the fishermen heard the news, they knew they had seen a phantom ship.

Oddly enough, the Fleming family had a previous ship, also called the *Nellie Flemming*, which shipped coal from the Bristol Channel ports to her home port of Youghal, County Cork. On a dark night of thick fog in 1913, she missed the lighthouse signal and ran aground on the Black Rock off Curragh in Ardmore Bay. That time no lives were lost, but the ship sank and the entire 250 ton load of coal was lost, later to be scavenged by the local people.

Some families, just like some nations, are cursed with bad luck.

Online Resources

Other mysterious titles by Charles River Editors

Other folk history titles by Charles River Editors

Other titles about the UK on Amazon

Further Reading

Adams, Paul and Peter Underwood. *Shadows in the Nave: A Guide to the Haunted Churches of England.* Stroud, Gloucestershire, United Kingdom: The History Press, 2011.

BBC News. "The Case of the Murdered Ghost." 3 January 2004. http://news.bbc.co.uk/2/hi/uk_news/england/london/3364467.stm Retrieved 2 October 2017.

Charles River Editors and Sean McLachlan. *Mysterious England: Monsters, Mysteries, and Magic Across the English Nation.* Charles River Editors, 2016.

Charles River Editors and Sean McLachlan. *Mysterious London: A History of Ancient Mysteries, Odd Individuals, and Unusual Legends across the English Capital.* Charles River Editors, 2016.

Green, Andrew. *Our Haunted Kingdom: more than 350 authenticated hauntings or case histories recorded in the UK over the past 25 years.* London, United Kingdom: Wolfe Publishing Ltd, 1973.

Ingram, John. *The Haunted Homes and Family Traditions of Great Britain.* London: Gibbings & Company, Ltd., 1897.

James, M.R. "Twelve Medieval Ghost-Stories" in *The English Historical Review*, Vol. 37, No. 147 (Jul., 1922), pp. 413-422.

Jones, Richard Glyn. *Haunted Castles of Britain and Ireland.* New York City, NY: Barnes & Noble Books, 2003.

Maple, Eric. *Supernatural England.* London: Robert Hale Ltd, 1977.

Marsden, Simon. *This Spectred Isle: A Journey through Haunted England.* New York City: Barnes & Noble, 2006.

Price, Harry. *The Most Haunted House in England: Ten Years' Investigation of Borley Rectory.* London, United Kingdom: Longmans, Green & Co., 1940.

Price, Harry. *The End of Borley Rectory.* London, United Kingdom: Harrap & Co., 1946.

Underwood, Peter. *Haunted London.* London: Amberly Publishing, 2010.

Westwood, Jennifer and Jacqueline Simpson. *The Lore of the Land: A Guide to England's*

Legends, from Spring-Heeled Jack to the Witches of Warboys. London: Penguin Publishing Company, 2005.

Wills, Keith. *Haunted Wiltshire.* Stroud, Gloucestershire: The History Press, 2014.

Wilson, Colin. *Poltergeist: A Classic Study in Destructive Hauntings.* Woodbury, MN: Llewellyn Publications, 2009.

Free Books by Charles River Editors

We have brand new titles available for free most days of the week. To see which of our titles are currently free, click on this link.

Discounted Books by Charles River Editors

We have titles at a discount price of just 99 cents everyday. To see which of our titles are currently 99 cents, click on this link.

Printed in Great Britain
by Amazon